GUIDE TO EFFECTIVE RISK MANAGEMENT 3.0

We would like to thank Alex Dali, Anthony Wilson, Mike Benke, Vincent Tophoff, Anna Korbut, Maxim Suharin, Dmitry Shevchenko, Lyubov Frolova, Linda Sidorenko, Konstantin Babaev, Roman Makeev, Pavel Viktorov, Ilya Oseev, Olga Obraztsova, Kira Nikolaichuk and Konstantin Dozhdikov for their help in writing this guide and making it as practical as possible.

SHORT QUESTIONNAIRE

This short questionnaire is designed to help risk managers mark their progress as they read through the guide and implement the recommendations provided within. It represents a simplified road map for the integration of risk management into the very culture and business processes of an organisation. Additional checklists and templates are provided throughout the document.

Mark the actions as you proceed:

OBJECTIVE 1: DRIVE RISK CULTURE

☐ Evaluate to what extent the company's strategy@risk

☐ Help set the tone at the top

☐ Document risk management roles and responsibilities

☐ Create a network of "risk-champions"

☐ Conduct risk management training

☐ Keep it simple

OBJECTIVE 2: HELP INTEGRATE RISK MANAGEMENT INTO BUSINESS

☐ Help employees integrate risk analysis into their daily work

☐ Make strategic planning, budgeting and performance management risk-based

☐ Promote open discussion about risks

OBJECTIVE 3: BECOME A TRUSTED ADVISOR

☐ Validate management assumptions

☐ Inform management about emerging risks

☐ Promote risk management as a service

☐ Take ownership over some risk assessments

☐ Build your own network of risk advisors

☐ Continuously improve your own risk management skills

CONTENTS

INTRODUCTION

Nowadays, risk management is on everyone's corporate agenda; let it be a private or public organisation. A special attention to risk management is paid by governments, stock exchanges, shareholders and regulators. However, this hasn't always been the case.

We began our risk management research back in 2007. This was the time when most large non-financial corporations were just starting to build risk management functions and implementing risk management frameworks. At the time, our study showed that risk management was largely driven by the stock exchange requirements and was very basic in nature.

We identified several challenges relating to weak risk culture and confusion around the roles and responsibilities that the boards, executives and the risk management teams play in the overall management of the company's risks. We also noted that back in 2007, risk managers focused primarily on foundation activities, such as developing risk management frameworks, conducting basic risk assessments and preparing risk reports that did not show a clear link between identified risks and corporate objectives. This resulted in very compliance-like and sometimes overly bureaucratic procedures. It often took months to get any meaningful results and it quickly became a box-ticking exercise. Business units resisted what was perceived as a "back office initiative," claiming that risks were already known and under control. All in all, risk management has failed to provide meaningful change to how companies operate or executives plan and make decisions.

It soon became apparent that there is a need for greater and more independent risk analysis and a link between risk management and business decision making. Management demanded risk analysis every time a decision was made, every day, not once a quarter or once a year. They wanted to see risk impact on their bottom line, cash flows, schedules and project NPV, not some abstract risk levels or heat maps. Unfortunately, most risk managers were not prepared for such new demands. Many tools and methodologies used by modern risk managers are simply not designed to provide a timely and quantitative assessment of risks related to everyday management decisions.

Today, as we continue to adapt to a highly volatile environment, businesses are becoming more proactive about risk management. Is this just a facade or are organisations truly becoming more risk aware?

During our research, we were pleasantly surprised by how many companies have already recognised the limitations of "stand-alone" and "separate" risk management processes and are proactive in integrating risk management into decision-making, core business processes and the overall culture of the organisation. We have collated best practices from more than a dozen mature organisations to propose an alternative approach to risk management. An approach without the heat maps, risk registers, risk frameworks or risk mitigation plans. For several years, we have tested and validated the findings both locally and internationally. Based on our research and the interviews, we have summarised fifteen practical ideas on how to improve the integration of risk management into the daily life of the organisation. These were grouped into three high level objectives: **drive risk culture**, **help integrate risk management into business** and **become a trusted advisor**.

This document is designed as a practical implementation guide. We recommend using it as such. Each section is accompanied by checklists, video references, useful links and templates.

OBJECTIVE 1: DRIVE RISK CULTURE

A. EVALUATE TO WHAT EXTENT THE COMPANY'S STRATEGY@RISK

Kevin W Knight, during his first visit to Russia a few years ago, said 'risk management is a journey... not a destination'*. Risk practitioners are free to start their journey at any point in this guide however the authors think that evaluating strategic objectives@risk can be considered a good starting point. The reason why we believe this is a good starting point is because it is relatively simple to implement, yet has an immediate and a significant impact on senior management decision making.

Before reading however, risk managers should start by having a frank discussion with their key stakeholders to try to understand what their expectations from risk management are. It is important to understand what their real appetite for change is.

Risk management is ultimately about changing organizational culture to accept risk and facilitate risk discussion when performing business activities or making any strategic, investment or project decisions. Vincent Tophoff in the recent International Federation of Accountants thought paper called **From Bolt-on to Built-in** has put it nicely "there is no such thing as risk culture. Instead, there is an organizational culture, in which managing risk should be an obvious, integrated action."

Below are some practical steps to integrate risk management into the overall culture of the organisation, make it part of the corporate DNA.

---

* https://www.scribd.com/document/283750131/A-Journey-Not-a-Destination-pdf

A1. Start by selecting the overall framework and documenting legal requirements

As far as international risk management standards go, the best choice for any non-financial organisation is by far the ISO 31000:2009. At the time of writing the standard had been officially translated and adopted in 44 out of 50 largest countries by GDP, making it truly global. ISO 31000:2009 is an international standard that provides principles and guidelines for effective risk management. It is not specific to any industry or sector and is intended to be tailored to meet the needs of the organisation. The standard is currently being reviewed by more than 200 risk professionals from 20+ countries from around the world. It is expected that the updated version, due to be published mid to late 2017, will provide greater emphasis on the need to integrate risk management into business activities and decision making and focus on the human and cultural aspects role in risk management.

Some industries have additional risk management related standards or guidelines. These are usually published by the industry associations, such as the Risk Management Guidelines developed by the European Private Equity & Venture Capital Association. And some countries, Germany for example, have specific laws and regulations related to risk management. All this additional guidance should be taken into account when implementing risk management in any given company.

The complexity and the risk management framework selected should be proportional to the size and risk profile of your business as well as the overall risk management maturity.

USE THE CHECKLIST PROVIDED BELOW TO TURN THIS SECTION INTO ACTIONS

☐ Check for country specific laws and regulations related to risk management

☐ Check for industry specific risk management guidelines or standards

☐ Familiarise yourself with the ISO31000:2009

☐ Get stakeholder buy-in on the selected risk management framework/standard

USEFUL VIDEOS

HOW TO SELL RISK MANAGEMENT TO EXECUTIVES?

A short video providing some suggestions on how to encourage senior management to implement risk-based thinking in the organisation.
https://www.youtube.com/watch?v=3MbJLkSlbU4

THE FUTURE OF RISK MANAGEMENT

In this video Alex Sidorenko talks about what the future of risk management holds for risk practitioners.
https://www.youtube.com/watch?v=yAiRWwYltdc

IS RISK MANAGEMENT A TOOL OR A PROFESSION?

Alex Sidorenko from RISK-ACADEMY discusses whether risk management is a profession or just a management tool.
https://www.youtube.com/watch?v=u9q6N8hr0qc

USEFUL LINKS AND TEMPLATES

- Roadmap for Risk Management Implementation - http://www.risk-academy.ru/en/download/roadmap-for-risk-management-implementation/

A2. Assess the effect of uncertainty on strategic objectives

Once the overall framework/standard is agreed upon and signed off by the key stakeholders, it is time to assess the effect of uncertainty on strategic objectives. Skip this section if the objectives have not been defined or documented in your company or if the objectives are not measurable.

STEP 1 - STRATEGIC OBJECTIVES DECOMPOSITION

Any kind of risk analysis should start by taking a high-level objective and breaking it down into more tactical, operational key performance indicators (KPIs) and targets. When breaking down any objectives it is important to follow the McKinsey MECE principle (ME - Mutually Exclusive, CE - Collectively Exhaustive) to avoid unnecessary duplication and overlapping. Most of the time strategic objectives are already broken down into more tactical KPIs and targets by the strategy department or HR, so this saves the risk manager a lot of time.

This is a critical step to make sure risk managers understand the business logic behind each objective and helps make risk analysis more focused.

Important note, while it should be management's responsibility to identify and assess risks, the business reality in your company may be that sometimes the risk manager should take the responsibility for performing risk assessment on strategic objectives and take the lead. Some of the ideas in this guide are quite controversial, because sometimes to make risk management work risk managers need to try different tactics not always aligned with "best practice" constantly published by consultants and regulators alike. We, of course, don't mean to compromise on ethics, we mean being agile and flexible in your thinking.

CONSIDER THE FOLLOWING EXAMPLE OF RISK MANAGEMENT IMPLIMENTATION

VMZ [†]– is an airline engine manufacturing business in Russia. Their product line consists of relatively old engines, DV30, which are used for the medium-haul airplanes Airliner 100. The production facility is in Samara, Russia. In 2012 a controlling stake (75%) was bought by an investment company AVIARUS.

During the last strategic Board meeting AVIARUS decided to maintain the production of the somewhat outdated DV30, although at a reduced volume due to plummeting sales and, more importantly, to launch a new engine, DV40, for its promising medium-haul aircraft Superliner 300.

The Board signed off on a strategic objective to reach an EBT (earnings before tax) of 3000 mln. rub. by the year 2018[‡].

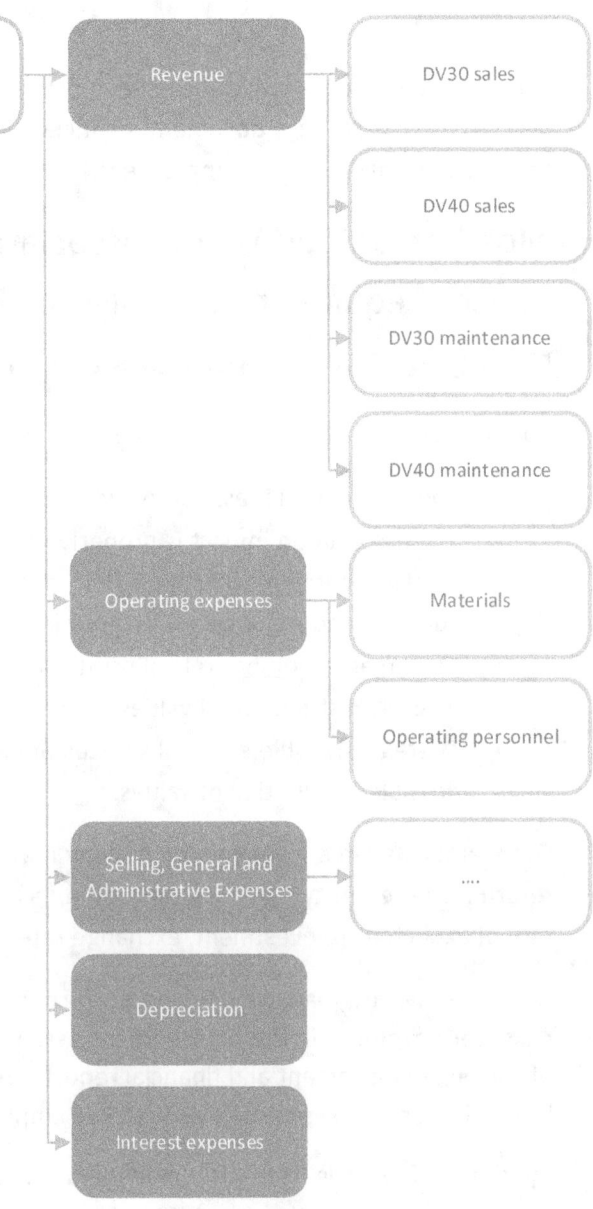

[†] Thank you, Konstantin Dozhdykov for creating and sharing sample risk modelling case study
[‡] In this case EBT was selected as an example only, it could be any value or metric used for decision making in your company, like Return on the Capital Invested or Return on Equity or any other measure.

Once the strategic objectives have been broken down into more tactical, manageable pieces, risk managers need to use the strategy document, financial model, business plan or the budgeting model to determine key assumptions made by the management.

Most assumptions are associated with some form of uncertainty and hence require risk analysis. Risk analysis helps to put unrealistic management assumptions under the spotlight.

Common criteria for selecting management assumptions for further risk analysis include:

- The assumption is associated with high uncertainty.
- The assumption impact is properly reflected in the financial model (for example, it makes no sense to assess foreign exchange risk if in the financial model all foreign currency costs are fixed in local currency and a change in currency insignificantly affects the calculation).
- The organisation has reliable statistics or experts to determine the possible range of values and the possible distribution of values.
- There are reliable external sources of information to determine the possible range of values and the possible distribution of values.

For example, a large investment company may have the following risky assumptions: the expected rate of return for different types of investment, an asset sale timeframe, timing and the cost of external financing, rate of expected co-investment, exchange rates and so on.

Concurrently, risk managers should perform a classic risk assessment to determine whether all significant risks were captured in the management assumptions analysis. The risk assessment should include a review of existing management and financial reports, industry research, auditors' reports, insurance and third party inspections, as well as interviews with key employees.

By the end of this step risk managers should have a **list of management assumptions**. For every management assumption identified, risk managers should work with the process owners, internal auditors and utilise internal and external information sources to determine the **ranges of possible values** and their likely **distribution shape**.

Macroeconomic assumptions	• Foreign exchange • Inflation • Interest rates (RUB) • Interest rates (USD)
Materials	• DV30 materials • DV40 materials
Debt	• Current debt • New debt
Engines sales	• New DV30 sales volume • New DV40 sales volume • DV30 repairs volume • DV40 repairs volume • DV30 price • DV40 price
Other expenses	• Current equipment and investments into new one • Operating personnel • General and administrative costs

Based on the management assumptions above, VMZ will significantly increase revenue and profitability by 2018. **Expected EBT in 2018 is 3013 mln. rub., which means the strategic objective will be achieved.**

We will review what will happen to management projections after the risk analysis is performed in the next section.

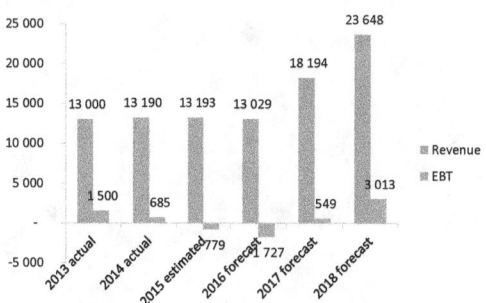

The next step includes performing a scenario analysis or the Monte-Carlo simulation to assess the effect of uncertainty on the company's strategic objectives. Risk modelling may be performed in a dedicated risk model or within the existing financial or budget model. There is a variety of different software options that can be used for risk modelling. All examples in this guide were performed using the Palisade @Risk software package, which extends the basic functionality of MS Excel or MS Project to perform powerful, visual, yet simple risk modelling.

When modelling risks it is critical to consider the correlations between different assumptions. One of the useful tools for an in-depth risk analysis and identification of interdependencies is a bow-tie diagram. Bow-tie diagrams can be done manually or using the Palisade Big Picture software. Such analysis helps to determine the causes and consequences of each risk, improves the modelling of them as well as identifying the correlations between different management assumptions and events.

The outcome of risk analysis helps to determine the risk-adjusted probability of achieving strategic objectives and the key risks that may negatively or positively affect the achievement of these strategic objectives. The result is strategy@risk.

The risk analysis shows that while the EBT in 2018 is likely to be positive, the probability of achieving or exceeding the strategic objective of 3000 mln. rub. is 4.6%. This analysis means:

- The risks to achieving the strategy are significant and need to be managed
- Strategic objectives may need to change unless most significant risks can be managed effectively

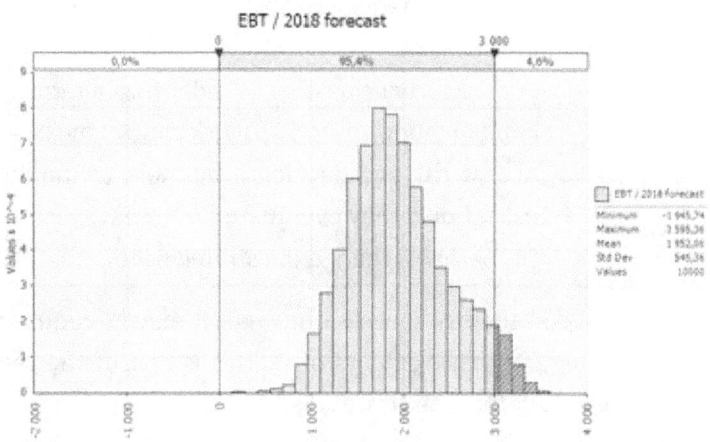

Further analysis shows that the volatility associated with the price of materials and the uncertainty surrounding the on-time delivery of new equipment have the most impact on the strategic objective.

Management should focus on mitigating these and other risks to improve the likelihood of strategic objective being achieved.

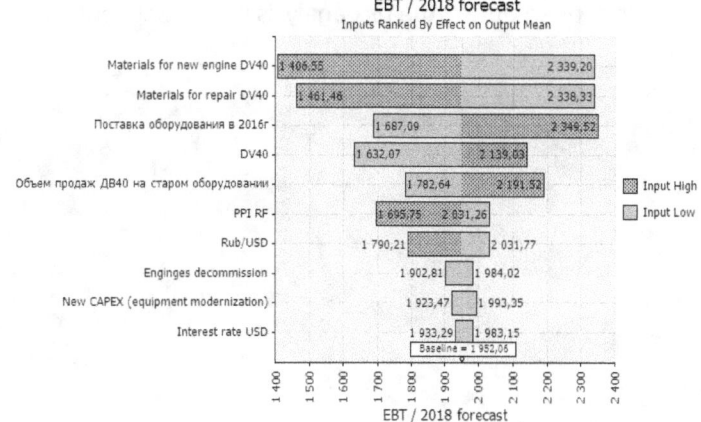

Tornado diagrams (right) and result distributions (top right) will soon replace risk maps and risk profiles as they much better show the impact risks have on objectives.

This simple example shows how management decision making process will change with the introduction of basic risk modelling.

Risk managers should discuss the outcomes of risk analysis with the executive team to see whether the results are reasonable, realistic and actionable. If indeed the results of risk analysis are significant, then the management with the help from the risk manager may need to:

- Revise the assumptions used in the strategy.
- Consider sharing some of the risk with third parties by using hedging, outsourcing or insurance mechanisms.
- Consider reducing risk by adopting alternative approaches for achieving the same objective or implementing appropriate risk control measures.
- Accept risk and develop a business continuity / disaster recovery plan to minimise the impact of risks should they eventuate.
- Or, perhaps, change the strategy altogether.

Based on the risk analysis outcomes it may be required for the management to review or update the entire strategy or just elements of it. This is one of the reasons why it is highly recommended to perform risk analysis before the strategy is finalised.

At a later stage the risk manager should work with the internal audit to determine whether the risks identified during the risk analysis are in fact controlled and the agreed risk mitigations are implemented.

USE THE CHECKLIST PROVIDED BELOW TO TURN THIS SECTION INTO ACTIONS

- [ ] Review existing strategy documents, business plans, financial or budget models to any management assumptions associated with significant uncertainty

- [ ] Perform classic risk assessment and add risks to the risk analysis if necessary

- [ ] Perform risk analysis using a scenario analysis or the Monte-Carlo simulation

- [ ] Present findings and conclusions to the management

- [ ] Adjust strategy based on risk analysis findings

- [ ] Audit strategy execution regularly

USEFUL VIDEOS

HOW TO QUANITIFY RISKS?

In this video, Alex Sidorenko talks about quantitative risk analysis and two possible ways to implement such analysis in an organisation.
https://www.youtube.com/watch?v=4fRAUZ4AD0I

IT SOLUTIONS FOR RISK MANAGEMENT. ANY GOOD ONES?

In this video, Alex Sidorenko talks about two types of risk management software as well as the pros and cons of each type.
https://www.youtube.com/watch?v=rGcwyrC2hDM

USEFUL LINKS AND TEMPLATES

- Risk identification questionnaire -
  http://www.risk-academy.ru/en/download/risk-identification-questionnaire/
- Sample bow-tie analysis -
  http://www.risk-academy.ru/en/download/bow-tie-risk-analysis/

B. HELP SET THE TONE AT THE TOP

B1. Develop a high-level Risk Management Policy

It is generally considered a good idea to document an organisation's attitude and commitment to risk management in a high-level document, such as a Risk Management Policy. The policy may describe the general attitude of the company towards risks, risk management principles, roles and responsibilities, risk management infrastructure as well as resources and processes dedicated to risk management. Section 4.3.2 of the ISO31000:2009 also provides guidance on risk management policy.

An article published by Michael Rasmussen back in October 2010 *'Enterprise Risk Management Policy Structure'* provides an outline of what should be included in a risk management policy and notes that the organisation's policy should not be "boilerplate." The policy should reflect the actual activities undertaken by the company and its attitude and approach to managing its material business risks.

USE THE CHECKLIST PROVIDED BELOW TO TURN THIS SECTION INTO ACTIONS

☐ Review ISO31000:2009 section 4.3.2

☐ Download a free sample Risk Management Policy from http://www.risk-academy.ru/en/download/risk management-policy-detailed/

☐ Adjust the sample Risk Management Policy to reflect organisational maturity and specific details

☐ Validate the policy with the stakeholders

☐ Approve it then publish it on the company website and make it accessible to employees and contractors

USEFUL VIDEOS

WHAT SHOULD A TYPICAL RISK MANAGEMENT FRAMEWORK INCLUDE?

What should a typical risk management framework include? Should an organisation develop a single integrated risk management framework document or is there a better way to integrate risk management into business processes and corporate culture?
https://www.youtube.com/watch?v=KMuhcmeJRgE

DO COMPANIES NEED A RISK MANAGEMENT POLICY?

Alex Sidorenko from RISK-ACADEMY talks about documenting and publishing a risk management policy.
https://www.youtube.com/watch?v=iFcOCXdTYfs

USEFUL LINKS AND TEMPLATES

- Sample Risk Management Policy (short version) - http://www.risk-academy.ru/en/download/risk management-policy-short/
- Sample Risk Management Policy (extended version) - http://www.risk-academy.ru/en/download/risk management-policy-detailed/

B2. Document risk appetite§ for different types of decisions

Most organisations have already documented their appetite for different common decisions or business objectives. Segregation of duties, financing and deal limits, procurement criteria, investment criteria, zero tolerance to fraud or safety risks – are all examples of how organisations set risk appetite. Appetite for different kinds of risks has been around for decades. Not all risks, but most of them.

So, what is this recent hype about risk appetite about? Not much really, it's just another consulting red herring. Contrary to what most modern day consultants tell us, the authors believe that any attempts in non-financial companies to aggregate risks into a single risk appetite statement is both unnecessary and unrealistic. Even having few separate risk appetite statements is totally missing the point.

After all, risk appetite is just a tool to help management make decisions and be transparent to stakeholders when making these decisions.

Instead of creating separate new risk appetite statements, risk managers should review existing Board level policies and procedures and identify:

- significant risks that already have its appetite set. For example, a company may have a Board level policy that prohibits any business ventures with organisations that utilise child labour. Or it may have a requirement not to invest in high risk ventures above a certain ratio. In cases, where the risk appetite has already been set, risk managers should work with internal auditors to test whether limits are realistic and are in fact adhered to;
- for the risks where no appetite has been set by any of the existing policies or procedures, the risk manager should work with the process owners to develop risk limits and incorporate them into existing policies and procedures. Main risks can be divided into three groups:
  - "Zero tolerance" risks.
  - Acceptable within quantitative limits.
  - Acceptable within qualitative limits.

We strongly believe that risk appetites should be integrated into existing Board level documents and very rarely, if ever, published as separate risk appetite statements.

In any case, appetite or tolerance for different types of risk should be reviewed periodically to remain current and applicable.

---

§ for the purposes of this guide the terms risk appetite, risk tolerance and risk limits are used interchangeably

USE THE CHECKLIST PROVIDED BELOW TO TURN THIS SECTION INTO ACTIONS

- ☐ Identify core decision making processes and the significant risks associated with these decisions

- ☐ Review existing Board level policies and procedures to check whether appetites for key risks have already been properly documented

- ☐ If not, update existing policies and procedures to include risk appetites / tolerances / limits

USEFUL VIDEOS

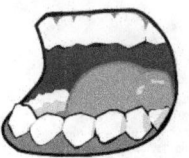

ALEX SIDORENKO TALKS TO RISKSTUDIO ABOUT RISK APPETITE

Interview with Alex Sidorenko on risk appetite and why it's totally overrated. Interview by Risk Studio.
https://www.youtube.com/watch?v=Kyj4x6re0hA

ARE RISK HEAT MAPS USEFUL?

Alex Sidorenko from RISK-ACADEMY talks about risk heat maps and why they are a complete waste of time. There are at least 3 better ways to present risk management information.
https://www.youtube.com/watch?v=XFwWLgKUJNQ

ARE RISK WORKSHOPS USEFUL?

Alex Sidorenko from RISK-ACADEMY speaks about how risk workshops are useful for education and awareness building, but not useful for risk identification and assessment.
https://www.youtube.com/watch?v=xT7ecliKUuY

USEFUL LINKS AND TEMPLATES

- Simple risk appetite evaluation for Board of directors -
  http://www.risk-academy.ru/en/download/evaluation-of-risk-appetite-on-the-board-of-directors/

B3. Include risk items on Board's agenda

This next step is very important to reinforce strong risk culture within the organisation. There are various ways of including risk discussion on the Board's agenda, however we believe that it is more effective to spend fifteen minutes on risk matters at every meeting than an hour once a quarter or a day once a year.

It is recommended to discuss risks associated with each decision instead of having risk management as a separate agenda item. After all items on Board's agenda are risk items.

For example, the Board may want to discuss risks associated with the quarterly budget when discussing the actual budget, or discuss project risks when approving project financing, as opposed to discussing the top ten corporate risks at the end of the meeting when all decisions have already been made.

The risk manager should, along with the Board secretary, make the necessary amendments to the presentation templates to include a section on risks for every significant decision. The risk manager, in conjunction with the internal audit, should also ensure that the risk information provided to the Board is complete, accurate and consistent. To improve the quality of such information, risk managers may wish to consider staff training or personally quality check the information before it goes to the Board.

Some Boards may create a separate Risk Committee or expand the scope of the Audit Committee to review matters related to risks. Our experience, when talking to different risk managers during the interviews, shows that this may be more fashionable than practical, since most decisions are taken long before the information is formally presented to the Board of Directors. Several people interviewed mentioned that it makes more practical sense to have a management level risk committee instead.

Nevertheless, the Board level risk committee can play an important oversight role and have a very positive impact on the overall risk culture within the organisation. Sometimes this is called "security theatre".

USE THE CHECKLIST PROVIDED BELOW TO TURN THIS SECTION INTO ACTIONS

☐ Update the Board presentation template to include risk analysis for every significant decision

☐ Discuss with the Board secretary the quality control process to ensure risk information is complete, accurate and consistent

☐ Train management to correctly and accurately disclose risks to the Board

☐ Control the quality of information disclosed

☐ Provide support to management in preparing risk information for the Board

USEFUL VIDEOS

INCLUDING RISK MANAGEMENT ON A BOARDS AGENDA

Alex Sidorenko from RISK-ACADEMY talks about various ways of including risk management information on the Board's agenda
https://www.youtube.com/watch?v=UBXw0cEPpws

ARE RISK REPORTS USEFUL?

Alex Sidorenko from RISK-ACADEMY talks about what risk reports are useful and how to integrate risk reporting into regular management reporting.
https://www.youtube.com/watch?v=AOGrobGzeaQ

USEFUL LINKS AND TEMPLATES

- Sample short risk report - http://www.risk-academy.ru/en/download/short-risk-report-presentation/
- Sample long risk report - http://www.risk-academy.ru/en/download/detailed-risk-report/
- Example of a completed risk register - http://www.risk-academy.ru/en/download/example-of-a-completed-risk-register/

B4. Consider establishing a Risk Management Committee at the management level or extend the mandate of the existing management committee

Most of the risk managers we have interviewed agreed that having a management level Risk Management Committee has a significant positive effect on the overall risk management culture.

While the composition of the Risk Management Committee can vary from company to company, it should be sufficiently representative to ensure different points of view on risk are considered. Based on our interviews, the best results tend to be achieved when the risk committee brings together supporting functions (finance, risk, legal, security, internal audit) and business units (operations, sales, marketing).

The Committee can either deal with matters related to risk management methodology or it may participate in the decision-making process (investments, projects and other high-risk activities) or both.

The Committee may meet on a regular basis (monthly or quarterly) as well as upon request from the Chairman of the Committee if there are questions that require urgent risk analysis.

USE THE CHECKLIST PROVIDED BELOW TO TURN THIS SECTION INTO ACTIONS

- ☐ Review the existing committees structure

- ☐ Decide on creating a new committee or extend the existing one

- ☐ Download an example of a Risk Management Committee charter from www.risk-academy.ru

- ☐ Decide on the Committee participation. Reward people for participation in the Risk Committee

- ☐ Develop a meeting schedule and make it available to employees

USEFUL VIDEOS

ARE RISK
COMMITTEES
USEFUL?

Alex Sidorenko from RISK-ACADEMY talks about the risk committees and whether they are useful for building risk culture and integrating risk management into decision making.
https://www.youtube.com/watch?v=fHwtr5pr1Rk

USEFUL LINKS AND TEMPLATES

- Risk Management Committee charter - http://www.risk-academy.ru/en/download/risk management-committee/

B5. Promote risk management within and outside the company

Risk managers need to learn to be proud of their contribution to the overall success of the company. Once the company achieves positive results by managing certain risks to a high standard, it is up to the risk manager to share this success both internally and externally. This can be done by presenting at various conferences and industry events or publishing small articles in relevant magazines or web publications. Here is a list of places where we normally publish our work:

- RISK-ACADEMY web portal www.risk-academy.ru/en/category/risk-articles-en
- G31000 LinkedIn discussion forum https://www.linkedin.com/groups/1834592
- Corporate Compliance Insights www.corporatecomplianceinsights.com
- Continuity Central www.continuitycentral.com
- CERM ® RISK INSIGHTS http://insights.cermacademy.com/
- Insurance Thought Leadership http://insurancethoughtleadership.com/

Sharing information about risk management in the company will raise risk management awareness internally and reinforce trust and transparency with suppliers, contractors, key clients and regulators externally. Clearly this is only applicable to non-confidential, public information that does not include any trade secrets or other sensitive information.

A number of the risk managers we have interviewed suggested that sharing information about risks and their mitigation with banks, investors, insurance companies and suppliers can result in significant cost savings on finance, insurance and the cost of goods.

Another good idea is to participate in annual risk management awards sessions, like the one organised by G31000 globally or by the Institute of Strategic Risk Analysis in Decision Making (ISAR) in Russia.

USE THE CHECKLIST PROVIDED BELOW TO TURN THIS SECTION INTO ACTIONS

- ☐ Publish regular risk management updates in internal news bulletins or email newsletters to staff

- ☐ Share success stories or useful tools or methodologies at local risk management conferences

- ☐ Participate in the global risk management discussion on G31000 LinkedIn group https://www.linkedin.com/groups/1834592

- ☐ Participate in the global risk management awards

USEFUL VIDEOS

CAN RISK MANAGEMENT MAKE SOME REAL MONEY?

Alex Sidorenko from RISK-ACADEMY talks about how a risk manager can help make real money for their company. Good risk managers can provide very tangible dollar savings and help raise new funds. Find out how in this short video. https://www.youtube.com/watch?v=cGZImxwDQBE

USEFUL LINKS AND TEMPLATES

- Publish a short risk management article on RISK-ACADEMY for free: http://www.risk-academy.ru/en/contact-us/

B6. Reinforce the "no blame" culture

Risk managers should encourage employees to openly raise risk management related issues. This is possible by spending a considerable amount of time every day communicating with their colleagues and staying up-to-date on the latest developments and emerging risks or failures in the internal control system.

Share the risk manager's contact information with employees or provide a confidential hotline for communicating risks through the internal company website or via the phone. Risk managers should motivate and encourage staff to be proactive about identifying and preventing risks. One of the risk managers we have interviewed started a table tennis tournament to build rapport with other business units and to have regular conversations in an informal setting with other managers.

Risk managers may consider introducing a rewards programme for active participation in risk management activities. It is important to encourage a "no blame" culture and communicate it throughout the company.

Another "unorthodox" option was to join forces with internal audit department and play "good cop, bad cop" with the business to drive the behaviour to reinforce better management of risks.

USE THE CHECKLIST PROVIDED BELOW TO TURN THIS SECTION INTO ACTIONS

☐   Reward open risk communication

☐   Encourage people to share information about risks by reaching out to them and by visiting their workplace regularly

☐   Participate in corporate team building activities and get to know local business units and the risks they are facing on a day to day basis

USEFUL VIDEOS

FOUR THINGS EVERY RISK MANAGER MUST KNOW

In this video, Alex Sidorenko talks about four critical skills that every risk manager must have to start on the risk management journey. It doesn't have to be one person with all four skills, it could be a team of people.
https://www.youtube.com/watch?v=nqmnycKZwgg

BUILDING STRONG RISK CULTURE

Alex Sidorenko from RISK-ACADEMY shares some of his practical suggestions on how to build a risk management culture.
https://www.youtube.com/watch?v=gafKiRlLGb0

USEFUL LINKS AND TEMPLATES

- Sample assessment of risk management culture - http://www.risk-academy.ru/en/download/risk management-culture-questionnaire/

B7. Join forces with the managers responsible for other areas of performance improvement

Risk managers should build relationships and join forces with the other managers responsible for performance improvement initiatives, like lean management, quality, safety, environment, security or others. Risk managers should participate in relevant major performance improvement workshops (for example, kaizen sessions during lean projects) to better understand sources of risks and suggested solutions, or at least review the results of those analytical sessions.

Risk managers should make sure that common risk management principles and language are used throughout the organization. However, they should be able to help tailor risk management tools for risks assessment and documentation to suit specifics of each function.

The ISO experts at the ISO Technical Committees level are doing it, making sure the language in ISO9001:2015 and ISO14000:2015 is consistent with ISO31000:2009, so no excuses for the risk managers on the ground.

USE THE CHECKLIST PROVIDED BELOW TO TURN THIS SECTION INTO ACTIONS

☐ Establish a temporary or permanent working group with managers responsible for other performance improvement initiatives

☐ Develop a roadmap for improving consistency in terms of principles and terminology in managing risks across different fields / siloes

USEFUL VIDEOS

BUILDING RISK MANAGEMENT ALLIANCES

Alex Sidorenko from RISK-ACADEMY talks about building alliances and collaborating with the managers responsible for the quality management system, safety and environmental management and others.
https://www.youtube.com/watch?v=pDEu2wAG4Yc

B8. Find the right sponsors

A large part of risk management success depends on the support and commitment from executives, Board members and key stakeholders.

It is important, as early as possible, to identify specific people at different levels within the organisation who support the concept of risk-based management and are ready to assist the risk manager:

- **At the executive level** – risk managers should find what motivates different executives, the CFO, for example, may be interested in implementing and supporting risk management to show the realistic risk-adjusted results and forecast to the banks and insurance companies to save on financing or insurance costs. Or he may be interested in having a methodology to validate investment projects, because he is not happy with how company was investing in very high risk initiatives lately. The COO may be interested to decrease the level of operational risks. The HR Director may be interested in timely identification of the staff turnover risk, etc.

- **At the Board level** – independent directors or other Board members may be supportive of risk management because it provides greater transparency in decision making and creates an additional information channel for them.

- **At the auditor level** – risk managers should participate in the audit methodology discussion and try to synchronise risk management methodologies between what is used internally and what external auditors apply.

- **At the regulator level** - risk managers should discuss regulators' expectations and methodologies to try to synchronise risk management methodologies between what is used internally and what regulators expect.

Finding the right sponsors is more of an art, than a science. It's highly unlikely that the risk manager will be able to convince all Board members or all executives. However, this is not really necessary, as long as the risk manager has support from certain individuals at every level mentioned above.

USE THE CHECKLIST PROVIDED BELOW TO TURN THIS SECTION INTO ACTIONS

Get executive sponsors on board to integrate risk management in the activities of a particular function.

☐ Help him / her realise potential benefits for the area of responsibility. Make him Chair of the Risk Management Committee (if it exists)

☐ Find interested parties at the Board level (try Audit Committee Chair or Independent Directors)

☐ Find support from an external auditor or regulator

USEFUL VIDEOS

FINDING THE RIGHT SPONSORS FOR RISK MANAGEMENT

Alex Sidorenko from RISK-ACADEMY talks about finding the right sponsors at the executive level, the Board of Directors and the external auditor and regulator level.
https://www.youtube.com/watch?v=NBJ04Dvj9Qo

WHO SHOULD THE RISK MANAGER REPORT TO?

Alex Sidorenko from RISK-ACADEMY talks about the place of the risk manager within the organisational structure, as well as the pros and cons of different reporting lines for the risk manager.
https://www.youtube.com/watch?v=r2b005LDwLA

HOW TO SELL RISK MANAGEMENT TO EXECUTIVES?

A short video providing some suggestions on how to encourage senior management to implement risk-based thinking in the organisation.
https://www.youtube.com/watch?v=3MbJLkSlbU4

CAN RISK MANAGEMENT MAKE SOME REAL MONEY?

Alex Sidorenko from RISK-ACADEMY talks about how a risk manager can help make real money for their company. Good risk managers can provide very tangible dollar savings and help raise new funds.
https://www.youtube.com/watch?v=cGZImxwDQBE

C. DOCUMENT THE RISK MANAGEMENT ROLES AND RESPONSIBILITIES

Documenting risk management roles and responsibilities is critical to building a sound organizational culture. The following five recommendations are designed to help embed risk management into the governance structure of the organisation.

C1. Select the risk governance model that best suits the current risk maturity level

The risk governance model depends on the management and shareholders' expectations as well as on the risk manager's competencies and on the resources available for risk management implementation.

The risk governance model can be built based on the classical concept of three lines of defence:

- The 1st line of defence - Business units: executives, business department management as well as employees. As part of their daily duties those listed above are responsible for timely identification, assessment, management, monitoring and reporting on risks. Senior management and the Board of Directors determine the strategy for risk management, approve risk appetite and monitor how major risks are managed.
- The 2nd line of defence - Functions of risk management and other support functions (such as safety and quality, finance, insurance, etc. are business consultants and are responsible for developing the methodology for managing risks, awareness and training, and methodological support. Sometimes the risk management team also performs a quality control function and aggregates information about the risks.
- The 3rd line of defence - Internal audit: Independent bodies, such as internal audit, provide independent monitoring that the risk management is carried out as in line with internal policies and procedures, and that the management of key corporate risks is performed.

While commonly accepted and simple in theory, the three lines of defence model is overly idealistic and doesn't work well in non-financial services. Risk managers may want to consider an alternative risk governance structure where:

- The risk management function is the centre of competence for all risk analysis and is responsible for an independent, timely and quantitative risk analysis for the decisions proposed by management. This model takes certain responsibilities from the traditional first line of defence, giving the risk managers greater responsibility and ownership over the risk analysis. This allows the risk manager to be directly involved in the process of decision making and to assume the responsibility for the outcomes on par with other executives.
- In certain cases, the risk manager may have the mandate to block excessively risky transactions or projects that do not meet the strategic goals of the company.

Based on the experience of the authors the second option is much more effective. Nassim Taleb calls it 'having the skin in the game'. To him, this is the only way to manage risks. We agree.

USE THE CHECKLIST PROVIDED BELOW TO TURN THIS SECTION INTO ACTIONS

☐ Propose different risk governance models for your organisation: one where the risk manager is passive and one where the risk manager is actively involved in the decision making

☐ Discuss risk governance models at the Risk Management Committee meeting

☐ Get stakeholder buy-in for the option selected

USEFUL VIDEOS

IS 3 LINES OF DEFENSE A USEFUL CONCEPT?

Alex Sidorenko from RISK-ACADEMY talks about whether the concept of 3 lines of defence is useful or not and how to make it work.
https://www.youtube.com/watch?v=INK2HIklZMM

WHAT IS THE ROLE OF THE MODERN RISK MANAGER?

Is it a methodology expert, a facilitator, an educator or a policeman? Maybe everything above? If so, in what proportion?
https://www.youtube.com/watch?v=hpix1vRb5wY

C2. Include risk management roles and responsibilities into existing job descriptions, policies and procedures, committee charters

Risk managers may begin the implementation of the selected risk governance model by documenting risk management roles and responsibilities. It is quite common to describe risk management roles and responsibilities in risk management policy or a framework document. This approach seems simple to implement, yet not very effective, as business units often don't feel ownership of these documents, instead they consider them irrelevant in everyday business and simply ignore them. There is a better way.

It is considered more effective to incorporate risk management roles and responsibilities into existing job descriptions, policies and procedures, various committee charters and working groups. Risk management roles and responsibilities must be identified and documented for all levels of management. As mentioned by a number of the risk managers we have interviewed, it is a much more effective than listing roles and responsibilities in the risk management policy or framework document.

Work with your HR team to include ISO31000 knowledge and risk management competencies in job descriptions / position descriptions for new hires.

USE THE CHECKLIST PROVIDED BELOW TO TURN THIS SECTION INTO ACTIONS

☐ Review existing job descriptions, committee charters, policies and procedures

☐ Update existing job descriptions, committee charters, policies and procedures to include risk management roles and responsibilities if not already done

☐ In order to reduce unnecessary tension, do the update in coordination with HR at the time when these documents are being reviewed anyway

☐ Include ISO31000 knowledge and risk management competencies in job descriptions for new hires

USEFUL VIDEOS

RISK MANAGEMENT ROLES AND RESPONSIBILITIES

Alex Sidorenko from RISK-ACADEMY talks about two ways of documenting risk management roles and responsibilities and the impact it has on risk culture.
https://www.youtube.com/watch?v=1Km332LJmPY

C3. Update existing policies and procedures to include elements of risk management

Most modern-day risk managers are familiar with developing a risk management framework or procedure documents. These documents capture risk management roles and responsibilities, outline risk management processes as well as other aspects of risk management. Risk management framework documents became so common, that nowadays they don't require much effort to develop and there are plenty of free templates available online. The only problem is that nobody in the organisation, except the risk manager and the internal auditor, reads them. Clearly, something is not right.

Over the years, we have discovered a much better way to document risk management frameworks, procedures and methodologies. Instead of writing a separate risk management framework, companies should upgrade its existing policies and procedures to include elements of risk management where appropriate. One investment company that we interviewed documented risk management methodology in the investment management procedure instead of creating any new risk management documents. This essentially changed how the investment process works, made risk management a critical step in investment decision making, gave investment managers a sense of ownership and had a huge positive impact on the risk culture within the organisation.

The same approach can also be used for any other business process. Instead of creating a single, centralised risk management framework or procedure document, risk managers should review and update existing policies and procedures to include elements of risk management. Some procedures may require a minor update, with only a sentence or two added while others may need whole appendices written to include risk management methodologies. This approach also reinforces the need to create separate risk management tools and methodologies for different business processes.

USE THE CHECKLIST PROVIDED BELOW TO TURN THIS SECTION INTO ACTIONS

☐ Identify existing policies and procedures associated with high uncertainty

☐ Review policies and procedures to determine if risk management is already adequately integrated

☐ Develop a timeline for updating existing policies and procedures to include elements of risk management

USEFUL VIDEOS

BUILDING STRONG RISK CULTURE

Alex Sidorenko from RISK-ACADEMY shares some of his practical suggestions to build risk management culture.
https://www.youtube.com/watch?v=gafKiRILGb0

WHAT SHOULD A TYPICAL RISK MANAGEMENT FRAMEWORK INCLUDE?

What should a typical risk management framework include? Should an organisation develop a single integrated risk management framework document or is there a better way to integrate risk management into business processes and corporate culture?
https://www.youtube.com/watch?v=KMuhcmeJRgE

C4. Regularly evaluate risk management culture

Every risk manager we have interviewed explained to us that periodic risk culture evaluations help strengthen the risk culture. So, we wanted to give readers some practical ideas around it.

There are multiple models which can be used to assess the current state of risk culture, including the risk culture framework developed by the Institute of Risk Management, UK or the risk maturity model developed by G31000 that covers elements of risk culture. Whatever the model risk managers select, they should make sure it is aligned with the ISO 31000:2009 principles.

When reviewing risk management culture, risk managers should, among other things, look at:

- **Whether accountabilities and responsibilities for risk are well documented -** A critical component of risk management integration is including responsibility and accountability (authority, resources, competences) for managing risks into all business activities. Top management should ensure that responsibilities and authority for relevant roles with respect to risk management are assigned and communicated at all levels of the organisation.
- **Evidence of risk management competencies** - Risk management competences should be developed in all core business units. Risk management competences should also become an important attribute when hiring new personnel to the organisation.
- **Evidence of risk management training and awareness** - All employees should receive risk management training appropriate to their level and risk exposure.
- **Whether individual performance management considers risk information** - Mature organisations align individual performance management with risk management. Employees should have individual key performance indicators relating to the management of risk and their participation in the risk management processes.
- **Evidence of open communication and transparency** - Information about the risks is openly discussed during the decision-making process. Significant risks are given due attention at the management and Board meetings. Executives are receptive to bad news and are ready to discuss risks and risk mitigations.

Risk managers should regularly discuss culture and attitude to risk with senior management and the Board, as well as help communicate Board and senior management expectations to the employees.

USE THE CHECKLIST PROVIDED BELOW TO TURN THIS SECTION INTO ACTIONS

- ☐ Choose the maturity model used to evaluate risk management culture (G31000, IRM, Risk-academy)

- ☐ Discuss with HR how to integrate risk culture evaluation into the regular employee surveys or broader organisational culture assessments

- ☐ Use online questionnaires and face-to-face interviews to assess risk culture maturity

- ☐ Monitor the progress at least once a year

USEFUL VIDEOS

BUILDING STRONG RISK CULTURE

Alex Sidorenko from RISK-ACADEMY shares some of his practical suggestions to build risk management culture. https://www.youtube.com/watch?v=gafKiRILGb0

USEFUL LINKS AND TEMPLATES

- Risk management culture assessment - http://www.risk-academy.ru/en/download/risk management-culture-questionnaire/

C5. Include risk management KPIs into individual performance reviews

Once risk management roles and responsibilities have been documented in job descriptions and committee charters then appropriate and measurable KPIs should be developed. Just like anything else, risk management KPIs need to be integrated into the overall performance management system.

Risk management is everyone's responsibility. Yet, our research shows that managing risks is not natural for people, it may even be against human nature. Without proper motivation or with inadequate motivation, employees are often reluctant to fulfil their risk management duties. This message was reinforced during our interviews. Companies that have implemented and monitored risk management KPIs for key employees have demonstrated significantly higher risk management culture maturity.

KPIs should be specific for each role within the overall risk governance model.

For example, KPIs for the CEO may include:

- an improvement in the risk management culture rating;
- regularity and quality of risk disclosure to shareholders;
- achieving risk-adjusted profitability measures.

For CFO or COO risk management KPIs may include:

- improvement in risk management culture maturity;
- RAROC (risk adjusted return on capital);
- the number of critical operational events and so on.

For the employees, a risk management KPI may include timely and accurate risk analysis during core business processes or significant decisions.

USE THE CHECKLIST PROVIDED BELOW TO TURN THIS SECTION INTO ACTIONS

- ☐ Review existing remuneration policy and individual performance KPIs for key decision makers

- ☐ Develop a set of KPIs for executives, risk managers, business unit heads and employees in high risk activities

- ☐ Together with HR and internal audit develop measurement / audit criteria for each KPI

- ☐ Pilot test on one business unit before a full roll-out

USEFUL VIDEOS

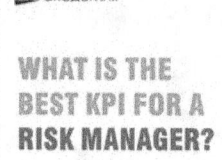 

Key performance indicators for risk managers - Alex Sidorenko from RISK-ACADEMY talks about various key performance indicators for risk managers
https://www.youtube.com/watch?v=4N3_eyaljbE

Omission bias: Alex Sidorenko talks about significant cognitive biases that affect how people in the workplace make decisions
https://www.youtube.com/watch?v=kh-bWQcF2RQ

COGNITIVE BIASES: NORMALCY BIAS

Normalcy bias: Alex Sidorenko talks about significant cognitive biases that affect how people in the workplace make decisions
https://www.youtube.com/watch?v=rIU4JGZjfxU

COGNITIVE BIASES: NEGLECT OF PROBABILITY

Neglect of probability bias: Alex Sidorenko talks about significant cognitive biases that affect how people in the workplace make decisions
https://www.youtube.com/watch?v=xhZ8HID4An4

COGNITIVE BIASES: DÉFORMATION PROFESSIONNELLE

Professional deformation bias: Alex Sidorenko talks about significant cognitive biases that affect how people in the workplace make decisions
https://www.youtube.com/watch?v=WfsP4stQtiU

COGNITIVE BIASES: SEMMELWEIS REFLEX

Semmelweis bias: Alex Sidorenko talks about significant cognitive biases that affect how people in the workplace make decisions
https://www.youtube.com/watch?v=kDbPMd4efOc

COGNITIVE BIASES: CONFIRMATION BIAS

Confirmation bias: Alex Sidorenko talks about significant cognitive biases that affect how people in the workplace make decisions
https://www.youtube.com/watch?v=P3GfC2mOgZI

COGNITIVE BIASES: FRAMING

Framing bias: Alex Sidorenko talks about significant cognitive biases that affect how people in the workplace make decisions
https://www.youtube.com/watch?v=bx3Or_cHHo8

D. CREATE A NETWORK OF "RISK-CHAMPIONS"

An active network of "risk champions" is a very effective management tool used to develop strong risk management culture. This network could become the "glue" between the risk management team and the rest of the business. "Risk champions" can be of three types:

- **Official risk coordinators** - employees, whose official duties include coordination of risk management processes within individual processes or business units. They are usually responsible for preparing information about risks, monitoring risk mitigation progress, organising risk management events or training.

- **Informants** – employees, who have established informal, yet trusted relationships with the risk managers. They provide information about emerging risks or changes in the organisation processes or risk profile. A large network of informants is critical for risk managers to stay up-to-date on what is happening in the company.

- **Influencers** – employees, who support the integration of risk management principles in the company's activities and processes because it makes good business sense for the company or them personally. They will usually participate in the Risk Management Committee meetings and will support initiatives proposed by the risk managers.

"Risk champions" help to implement risk management elements in key business processes and procedures within the organisation. Usually, "risk-champions" are employees who are naturally motivated to effectively manage risks, such as employees responsible for project management, methodology, process improvement etc. For larger organisations, it may be necessary to identify "risk-champions" not only for key processes, but also for each geographical area where the company is represented.

USE THE CHECKLIST PROVIDED BELOW TO TURN THIS SECTION INTO ACTIONS

- ☐ Determine significant business processes where risk management will be integrated first

- ☐ Identify key middle level employees across selected business processes to provide risk management awareness training

- ☐ Involve "risk champions" in risk management activities or Risk Management Committee meetings

- ☐ Provide ongoing support to "risk champions"

- ☐ Informally find people within the company who appreciate the value of risk management. Develop relationships with them and involve them in risk management activities

USEFUL VIDEOS

DO COMPANIES NEED RISK CHAMPIONS?

Alex Sidorenko from RISK-ACADEMY talks about creating risk champions and the two different kinds of risk champions
https://www.youtube.com/watch?v=dOgJ9zJfy8I

E. CONDUCT RISK MANAGEMENT TRAINING

Risk management may seem simple enough in theory, but not all employees have the necessary skills and competencies to successfully apply it in practice. One of the key components in driving change is employee training and development.

E1. Include the principles of risk-based decision-making in induction training for new employees

New hires come from a variety of education and experience backgrounds and most importantly, each new employee has their own perception of what is an acceptable risk. It is important for risk managers to cooperate with the Human Resources department or any other business unit responsible for training, to jointly carry out training on the basics of risk management for all new employees.

One of the risk managers we interviewed mentioned that the risk management induction should not be long. It should take about ten minutes and include the basics of business and investment decisions under uncertainty, key risk management roles and responsibilities and the ISO31000:2009 risk management principles as per the company's Risk Management Policy.

Examples of free risk management training slides can be found at
https://www.risk-academy.ru/en/download/free-risk-slides-for-trainers/

USE THE CHECKLIST PROVIDED BELOW TO TURN THIS SECTION INTO ACTIONS

☐ Review existing induction programmes for new employees

☐ Discuss with HR whether to develop a new induction training dedicated to risk management or include risk management messages in existing inductions

☐ Deliver induction training face to face or record an online risk management induction course

☐ Consider hiring RISK-ACADEMY to develop an online risk management induction programme for you. The company can be found at http://www.risk-academy.ru/en/corporate-risk-management-training

USEFUL VIDEOS

RISK MANAGEMENT TRAINING AND AWARENESS

Alex Sidorenko from RISK-ACADEMY talks about four ways to deliver risk management training within a corporation
https://www.youtube.com/watch?v=ZojnD4c3JqQ

E2. Conduct training for senior management and the Board

Tone at the top is very important for risk culture development. Executives and Board members play a vital role in driving the risk management agenda. Nowadays many executives and Board members have a basic understanding of risk management. Auditors, risk management professional associations and regulators have been quite influential in shaping the Board's perception of risk management.

Unfortunately, not all the messages communicated by the auditors and regulators are sound and some are downright wrong. For example, one of the government agencies in Russia published a guidance document that encourages companies to have a standalone risk management process and in many ways contradict the core principles of ISO31000:2009.

It is important for the risk manager to take the lead on forming the Boards and senior managements view on risk management by providing risk awareness sessions and relevant information. Here are some of the most important messages risk managers need to include in their communication with the Board:

- Decision quality and how people make decisions under uncertainty;
- Positioning risk management as a tool to help management make decisions;
- Risk management should be an integral part of existing business processes and regular management reporting, not a standalone quarterly or annual activity;
- Risk management is not about avoiding or minimising risks, it's about making informed decisions.

It may be appropriate to bring in an independent advisor to conduct risk awareness training for the Boards and senior management to reinforce the messages shared by the risk managers internally.

USE THE CHECKLIST PROVIDED BELOW TO TURN THIS SECTION INTO ACTIONS

- ☐ Discuss with HR the best options to conduct risk management awareness training for the Board and senior management. Conduct war games or use other gamification techniques

- ☐ Conduct risk management awareness training that covers risk psychology (cognitive biases), decision quality and risk management integration at least annually

- ☐ Include risk awareness sessions/topics on the agenda of the regular Board meeting or strategy sessions

- ☐ Include risk management competencies in the Board performance assessment criteria (if applicable)

USEFUL VIDEOS

Alex Sidorenko from RISK-ACADEMY talks about the ultimate objective for risk management
https://www.youtube.com/watch?v=QOiks_T7EyQ

Short video on the use of various gamification techniques to train employees in managing risks
https://www.youtube.com/watch?v=EdgbdOE-yCY

E3. Conduct training for "risk-champions"

Provide additional risk management training to the in-house risk management team and business units responsible for internal control, audit, finance, strategy and others. Risk managers may conduct it personally or outsource to third party providers. In-depth risk management training should include (this example is based on the actual risk management training provided by Institute for Strategic Risk Analysis in Decision Making (ISAR) and RISK-ACADEMY):

RISK MANAGEMENT FOUNDATIONS
- Definition of risk
- History of risk management
- International and national risk management standards
- Introduction to finance, project management and process management
- Introduction to statistics
- Insurance basics

RISK MANAGEMENT IN DECISION MAKING
- Identification of risks associated with decision making or goals/KPIs achievement
- Risk analysis in decision making (sensitivity analysis, scenario analysis, Monte-Carlo simulations, decision trees, scoring models)
- Risk mitigation and risk-based decision making
- Disclosure, reporting, monitoring and review

PSYCHOLOGY AND RISK MANAGEMENT CULTURE
- Risk psychology and cognitive biases in decision making
- Risk management culture
- Principles of risk management ethics

INTEGRATING RISK MANAGEMENT INTO THE BUSINESS
- Understanding the organisational appetite for risk
- A roadmap for risk management integration:
  - Developing new and updating existing policies and procedures
  - Integration into decision making, planning, budgeting, purchasing, auditing etc.
  - Risk management roles and responsibilities, risk management KPIs
  - Integrating risk information into management reporting
  - Resources required for the implementation of risk management
- Auditing risk management effectiveness
- Risk management continuous improvement
- Risk management software

For more information about training programmes or to order training for your company see www.risk-academy.ru/en/corporate-risk-management-training. If you are interested in sitting the G31000 certification exam after the training and receiving a risk management certification, please refer to http://www.risk-academy.ru/en/c31000-risk management-certification/

USE THE CHECKLIST PROVIDED BELOW TO TURN THIS SECTION INTO ACTIONS

☐ Identify key stakeholders within the organisation who may benefit from advanced risk management training

☐ Provide in-depth risk management training for risk champions that covers the key principles of ISO31000:2009, decision quality and cognitive biases, risk quantification, risk culture and integration of risk analysis into decision making and core processes

USEFUL VIDEOS

WHICH RISK MANAGEMENT CERTIFICATION TO CHOOSE

Alex Sidorenko talks about 3 things to consider when choosing a risk management certification programme. He also talks about different certification options that are currently available in the market.
https://www.youtube.com/watch?v=bvV41BrqKmg

RISK MANAGEMENT TRAINING AND AWARENESS

Alex Sidorenko from RISK-ACADEMY talks about four ways to deliver risk management training within a corporation.
https://www.youtube.com/watch?v=ZojnD4c3JqQ

3 THINGS TO INCLUDE IN ANY RISK MANAGEMENT TRAINING

Alex Sidorenko from RISK-ACADEMY talks about 3 important things that must be included in any risk management training
https://www.youtube.com/watch?v=vLvz3SE8AI0

E4. Make risk training competency based

Just like any other business expense, a risk management training budget needs to be justified. And just like any investment decision, risk management training needs to show adequate return on investment. Training costs money: the development process, hiring trainers and getting employees to dedicate time away from their workplace to participate in training.

One useful way, suggested by risk managers we interviewed, was to make all risk management training competency based and setting KPIs to check for noticeable improvement in the quality of risk based decision making. Each training session should start and end with competency tests. Surveys should also be conducted one month and six months after the training to test for knowledge retention.

USE THE CHECKLIST PROVIDED BELOW TO TURN THIS SECTION INTO ACTIONS

- ☐ Develop a short risk management questionnaire to distribute to employees before training to test current level of knowledge

- ☐ Develop a set of questions to test risk management knowledge directly after the training or throughout the training

- ☐ Develop short tests to validate risk management knowledge 3 or 6 months after the training

- ☐ Make tests gradable and reward participants who show best in class performance

USEFUL VIDEOS

RISK MANAGEMENT TRAINING AND AWARENESS

Alex Sidorenko from RISK-ACADEMY talks about four ways to deliver risk management training within a corporation.
https://www.youtube.com/watch?v=ZojnD4c3JqQ

3 THINGS TO INCLUDE IN ANY RISK MANAGEMENT TRAINING

Alex Sidorenko from RISK-ACADEMY talks about 3 important things that must be included in any risk management training
https://www.youtube.com/watch?v=vLvz3SE8AI0

E5. Develop certification programmes for employees in high risk activities

Another useful suggestion is to develop an internal risk management certification for employees working in high-risk activities. This will ensure staff working in high risk activities, like manufacturing, trading, insurance, security and others possess adequate risk management skills and remain cognisant of the risks associated with their work.

Certification programmes may be developed internally or outsourced. Depending on the high-risk activity the certification may be high level or in-depth, in any case it should test:

- Understanding of legal obligations;
- Awareness of risks in the workplace;
- Ability to make quality decisions under uncertainty;
- Understanding the protocol for communicating and escalating risks;
- Evidence of moral and ethical behaviour.

USE THE CHECKLIST PROVIDED BELOW TO TURN THIS SECTION INTO ACTIONS

☐ Identify high-risk areas in the workplace

☐ Discuss with HR the possibility of an internal certification programme for high-risk activities

☐ Develop an internal certification programme together with the employees working in high-risk activities and external experts

USEFUL VIDEOS

WHICH RISK MANAGEMENT CERTIFICATION TO CHOOSE

Alex Sidorenko talks about 3 things to consider when choosing a risk management certification programme. He also talks about different certification options that are currently available in the market.
https://www.youtube.com/watch?v=bvV41BrqKmg

E6. Use passive learning techniques

Make sure that risk management information is available to employees, contractors and visitors. Place Risk Management Policy on the intranet and the corporate website, record and publish risk management training or awareness sessions videos on the dedicated risk management intranet page.

Invite guest speakers (risk managers from other companies) to speak at the Audit Committee or Risk Management Committee and give employees the opportunity to participate. We have used this in the past and it worked very well.

Periodically post useful risk management related articles and research papers on the corporate intranet. Make the risk management information easily accessible to staff.

USE THE CHECKLIST PROVIDED BELOW TO TURN THIS SECTION INTO ACTIONS

- ☐ Create a dedicated risk management page on the corporate intranet site

- ☐ Record risk management training on video

- ☐ Publish training videos, templates, useful materials and ISO31000 related materials on the corporate intranet

- ☐ Give all employees access to the corporate risk management webpage

USEFUL LINKS AND TEMPLATES

- Sample risk management policy (detailed version) http://www.risk-academy.ru/en/download/risk management-policy-detailed/
- Sample risk management policy (short version) http://www.risk-academy.ru/en/download/risk management-policy-short/
- Free risk management training slides http://www.risk-academy.ru/en/download/free-risk-slides-for-trainers/

F. KEEP IT SIMPLE

The golden rule of risk management - the simpler it is, the more transparent and easier it is to understand and implement!

The Risk manager's goal should be helping organisations become more risk-based. Risk management tools and methodologies should be clear to the rest of the organisation and easily adoptable in the normal course of doing business. Otherwise risk managers are likely to meet a lot of resistance or be simply ignored, which is even worse.

Risk managers need to speak the business language and avoid the risk management jargon when dealing with the business. The use of the terms VaR, EaR, CFaR may be perfectly acceptable to communicate with the CFO, but the Head of production will very quickly lose interest. Even the most basic terms like risk profile, risk mitigation, risk owner, risk assessment are unnecessary and completely avoidable.

USE THE CHECKLIST PROVIDED BELOW TO TURN THIS SECTION INTO ACTIONS

☐ Regularly sanity check your risk management methodologies. If they are not understood by the business they will not be adopted

USEFUL VIDEOS

Alex Sidorenko from RISK-ACADEMY talks about keeping it simple and not overcomplicating risk management implementation.
https://www.youtube.com/watch?v=h4o4OgubD1c

OBJECTIVE 2: HELP INTEGRATE RISK MANAGEMENT INTO BUSINESS

G. HELP EMPLOYEES INTEGRATE RISK ANALYSIS INTO THEIR WORK

Over the years, risk managers have tried various ways to get the business units to participate in the risk management process. Some simplified the risk identification and assessment methodologies, others complicated them. The result in both cases was the same - disappointment. Best case scenario - annual or quarterly risk assessments were perceived as a necessary evil with most employees ignoring them and few actively resisting. In this guide the authors are proposing an alternative approach. Something that will help integrate risk management into everything the business does.

Did it ever strike you as odd, that risk management is supposed to be a support function, yet business units are constantly required to provide the information to the risk managers and not the other way around? It almost feels like the business is there to support risk managers in doing their job.

Maybe, just maybe, it is time for the risk managers to stop living in a universe, where the business is regularly required to provide information, participate in risk assessments and to contribute to lengthy discussions about risk mitigation. After all, this does not make business sense. Why would business units take the time away from making money to supply risk managers with all this information? The only logical answer is because they must, it's a compliance issue. And this is where it gets interesting, risk managers have for years been telling us that it's not about compliance, it's about generating business value. Something doesn't add up. If an activity takes time and resources and doesn't have an immediate impact on business decisions or business processes, something is clearly wrong.

This guide is designed to help the business take risks into account every time they take a decision, not quarterly or annually. The authors believe that this can only be achieved by changing the very nature of existing business processes (planning, budgeting, investment management, performance management, procurement and so on) and making them more risk-based. This also means that risk management process is not a singular process, there should be multiple, different risk management processes in the organisation.

USE THE CHECKLIST PROVIDED BELOW TO TURN THIS SECTION INTO ACTIONS

☐ Critically review existing risk management processes and methodologies to determine whether they do in fact help management make day to day business decisions based on timely and accurate risk information

☐ Document risk information flows in the company to make sure risk management provides adequate and timely support to all business units

USEFUL VIDEOS

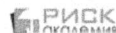

WHAT IS THE ULTIMATE GOAL OF RISK MANAGEMENT?

Alex Sidorenko from RISK-ACADEMY talks about the ultimate objective for risk management
https://www.youtube.com/watch?v=QOiks_T7EyQ

WILL THE ROLE OF THE RISK MANAGER CHANGE?

Alex Sidorenko from RISK-ACADEMY talks about how will the role of the risk manager will change over the next few years
https://www.youtube.com/watch?v=IubYqCFiJ2c

H. RISK-BASED STRATEGIC PLANNING, BUDGETING AND PERFORMANCE MANAGEMENT

According to the ISO 31000:2009, principles risk management should be an integral part of organisational processes and decision making. Picking up on that important point, risk management should be seen as a management tool designed to improve planning, budgeting, performance management and other core business processes. Risk management also helps management to make more informed business decisions about achieving strategic or operational goals and sometimes may even highlight the need to change the strategy altogether due to an unacceptable level of risk.

Below are just some of the practical ideas to help integrate risk management:

- Document appetites / tolerances for different risk types in the relevant Board level policies and procedures instead of creating separate risk appetite statements;
- Identify significant risks and assess their impact on the Company's business plan and budget;
- Run risk simulation to determine realistic strategic or operational KPI values;
- Run risk simulation to determine key budget constraints;
- Integrate risk analysis into key management, investment and project decisions;
- Remunerate management based on risk-adjusted performance measures.

Effective risk management increases management confidence in achieving objectives, reduces uncertainty and helps make informed, risk-based decisions. In this section, we provide examples of how risk management can be integrated into:

H1. Strategic planning;
H2. Budgeting;
H3. Performance management;
H4. Decision making.

H1. INTEGRATION INTO STRATEGIC PLANNING

We start with strategic planning because it affects all levels of management, hence giving maximum exposure to risk management. Senior management, Board members and even some shareholders input into the process, while the rest of the company and broader stakeholders usually see the outputs of strategic planning. Integrating risk management into strategic planning helps to raise the risk management awareness and address the uncertainty associated with achieving strategic objectives.

The impact of uncertainty on the strategic objectives should be assessed at the time the strategy is formulated and not after it was approved by the Board of Directors. To integrate risk management into strategic planning properly, risk managers first need to build the relationship with the strategic planning department then make sure the strategic risks are included on the strategic sessions / workshops agenda and provide risk analysis to support such discussions. Another action point is to include elements of risk analysis into the actual strategy setting and update processes. Risk managers can use scenario analysis or simulation modelling to present an independent opinion on strategic objectives and the impact the risks may have on their achievement.

In some cases, the company's senior management or Board members may request an in-depth analysis of certain strategic risks before finalising the strategy. One of the risk managers we interviewed told us how analysing long-term liquidity using the Monte-Carlo simulation helped reshape the whole strategy of the company.

USE THE CHECKLIST PROVIDED BELOW TO TURN THIS SECTION INTO ACTIONS

☐ Include risk management as an agenda item for the next strategy session

☐ Review the existing strategic plan to see whether risks and their mitigations are adequately covered

☐ Test whether strategic assumptions are realistic, adequate and give sufficient consideration to risks. Perform scenario analysis or simulation modelling to test the validity of management assumptions

☐ Perform in-depth risk analysis on the most significant strategic risks to test their impact on the strategy

☐ Document the requirements to capture and mitigate strategic risks into the policies and procedures. Make risk analysis part of the strategic planning process

USEFUL VIDEOS

MAKING BUSINESS PROCESSES RISK BASED

Alex Sidorenko from RISK-ACADEMY talks about making the risk management process risk -based and answers a question on where to start with the risk management implementation.
https://www.youtube.com/watch?v=eEPHjfTGh2Q

H2. INTEGRATION INTO BUDGETING

While it is quite common to budget using three scenarios (optimistic, realistic and pessimistic) it may not be sufficient from a risk management point of view. These scenarios are often formed without the risk management team's participation or even without due consideration of the actual risks, associated with the budget. Thus, even the pessimistic scenarios often do not account for many significant risks, creating an overly optimistic and misleading picture for the executives and decision-makers.

Proper risk analysis can bring significant value to the budgeting process. Risk managers should review and improve management assumptions used in scenario analysis or introduce the use of simulation modelling to make sure all important risks are captured and their impact on liquidity assessed. Risk analysis helps replace static, point in time, budgets with a distribution of possible values. It also helps set management KPIs based on the risk information, thus improving the likelihood of them being achieved and reduces the conflict of interest the finance department and management team have in presenting an overly optimistic budget. Risk analysis helps to identify the most critical risks affecting the budget, allowing management to allocate ownership and determine the budget for risk mitigation.

Integrating risk management into the budgeting process requires the risk management team working closely with the finance department, as risk analysis may lead to the change in budget assumptions or targets.

USE THE CHECKLIST PROVIDED BELOW TO TURN THIS SECTION INTO ACTIONS

☐ Review existing policies and procedures covering budgeting process to determine whether risks are adequately taken into account

☐ Test the existing budget model using sensitivity or scenario analysis to determine whether risks are adequately covered

☐ Perform simulation modelling on the budget model to determine the likelihood of objectives being achieved as well as to identify any liquidity problems

☐ Determine the most significant risks that affect the budget and risk mitigation measures

☐ Adjust the budget based on risk information

USEFUL VIDEOS

Alex Sidorenko from RISK-ACADEMY talks about making the risk management process risk -based and answers a question on where to start with the risk management implementation.
https://www.youtube.com/watch?v=eEPHjfTGh2Q

H3. INTEGRATION INTO PERFORMANCE MANAGEMENT

Risk management should be integrated into the performance management cycle of the organisation: both at the individual level and the corporate level.

One of the risk managers we interviewed shared an example where traditional static corporate key performance indicators (KPIs) have been replaced with dynamic, risk-based, ranged KPIs. This allowed their management to have bands of values instead of a single value. Some KPIs stayed as single value estimates however they were calculated as the 95% percentile of the distribution of possible values based on the Monte-Carlo simulation. Triggers and key risk indicators may also be set for corporate KPIs to improve monitoring and performance tracking.

At an individual level, risk management KPIs may be set around risk-based decision making, timely risk mitigation, risk management training grades or an internal audit assessment of the risk management effectiveness in different business units. For more information on individual risk management KPIs please refer to C5. Include risk management KPIs into individual performance reviews.

USE THE CHECKLIST PROVIDED BELOW TO TURN THIS SECTION INTO ACTIONS

- ☐ Review existing methodology used to calculate strategic and operational KPIs

- ☐ Test whether KPIs are calculated based on appropriate risk analysis or whether current targets are overly optimistic and ignore risks

- ☐ Develop a set of corporate risk management or risk-based KPIs to raise risk management awareness

- ☐ Develop a set of individual KPIs for key managers to raise risk management awareness and assign responsibility

USEFUL VIDEOS

MAKING BUSINESS PROCESSES RISK BASED

Alex Sidorenko from RISK-ACADEMY talks about making the risk management process risk -based and answers a question on where to start with the risk management implementation.
https://www.youtube.com/watch?v=eEPHjfTGh2Q

WHAT IS THE BEST KPI FOR A RISK MANAGER?

Key performance indicators for risk managers - Alex Sidorenko from RISK-ACADEMY talks about various key performance indicators for risk managers
https://www.youtube.com/watch?v=4N3_eyaljbE

H4. INTEGRATION INTO DECISION-MAKING PROCESSES

Risk management should not be viewed as a separate, stand-alone process. One of the most effective and yet simple ways to change management's perception about risk management is to integrate risk analysis into the various decision-making processes.

Performing risk assessments for all significant business decisions can dramatically raise decision quality and provide management with valuable insight and alternatives. This statement alone has great implications for modern-day risk management. Business decisions are made daily, not monthly or quarterly when risk managers usually refresh their risk assessments. Risk management processes should change to accommodate this business demand.

Another important question is - who should be responsible for the quality and timeliness of risk analysis for each decision. Should it be the business units, risk owners who initiate the decision or an independent risk manager? Despite the widely-accepted model of three lines of defence, the choice is not always obvious. While the authors are confident that risk analysis should be integrated in the decision-making process, the scope and complexity of each decision should determine the extent of the necessary risk analysis, the tools used and the responsible party. This was covered in C1. Select the risk governance model that best suits the current risk maturity level.

To help integrate risk management into decision-making, risk managers may consider making changes to the current templates which are used for presenting decisions to senior management and the Board. Including a simple section called "risks associated with the proposed decisions and risk mitigation" can help raise risk awareness, reinforce the need for timely risk analysis and improve risk disclosure. This was covered in B3. Include risk items on Board's agenda.

Other examples may include:

- **Investment decisions.** Using simulation modelling to assess the investment attractiveness of projects can allow the company to avoid many pitfalls associated with more traditional valuation methods. Instead of the net present value (NPV) assessment, companies can estimate distribution of possible outcomes, the probability of a negative NPV and most significant risks that need to be mitigated to improve project performance. Scenario analysis and simulations can significantly improve the quality of the investment analysis.
- **Assessing behavioural risks.** Use elements of game theory and behavioural psychology to improve the quality of risk analysis, identify trends and, consequently, increase the quality of business decisions. Additional material on game theory can be found at www.patrickmcnutt.com
- **Financing decisions.** Most financing decisions involve a trade-off between risk (potential cost) and potential benefit. Very often these decisions are based on expert opinions and assumptions, instead of the proper analysis of cash flow at risk or other risk-based financial indicators.
- **Operational decisions.** Decisions on production forecasts, supply chain, plant maintenance, outsourcing and inventory also require a balanced analysis of risk and return.

USE THE CHECKLIST PROVIDED BELOW TO TURN THIS SECTION INTO ACTIONS

☐ Review a sample of past significant business decisions to see whether information about risks relevant to the decision was captured, analysed and disclosed

☐ Determine which business decisions regularly taken by the management may benefit most from additional risk analysis

☐ Develop a methodology that will allow risk assessments to be carried for every significant business decision before the decision is taken

☐ Quality control the results of risk analysis used during decision making

USEFUL VIDEOS

WHAT IS THE ULTIMATE GOAL OF RISK MANAGEMENT?

Alex Sidorenko from RISK-ACADEMY talks about the ultimate objective for risk management
https://www.youtube.com/watch?v=QOiks_T7EyQ

I. PROMOTE OPEN DISCUSSIONS ABOUT RISKS

I1. Speak the business language

Bryan Whitefield said it best in his newsletter: 'Identify all the stakeholders you need to influence. Identify the order in which you wish to tackle them. It is always best to get senior management's buy-in first; however, sometimes that just isn't possible, and you have to win over their key influencers before you can tackle them. Make sure you have a clear strategy. Identify their main motivators, hobbies, and interests. Your best opportunity for engaging someone who does not already know you and trust you is to ignite his/her interest through something he/she is already passionate about.

Risk management has so many intangibles. You need to do your best to make what you want to achieve seem tangible to your target audience. People comprehend best when you provide them with both visual and verbal descriptions—so draw a picture and tell a story. Choose examples that are most likely to relate to the motivators, hobbies, and interests you have identified.

Speak their language—I call it moving from "risk speak" to "c-suite speak" when engaging senior executives. Too often we simply blurt out what we know is needed in what we might consider to be simple risk language; however, it may mean almost nothing to our audience. Try talking "inherent risk" with a CEO. You know—the world without controls. You would probably agree that a better approach would be to discuss the need to identify where the organisation may be able to save some compliance costs by understanding which of the company's current controls are the most important and which are not.'

Source: Risk e-Views Vol 4, December 2010, Risk Leadership: How to be Heard, Bryan Whitefield, Director, Risk Management Partners (reproduced with the permission of the author).

USE THE CHECKLIST PROVIDED BELOW TO TURN THIS SECTION INTO ACTIONS

☐ Speak about risks in terms of their impact on achieving or not achieving business objectives

☐ Discuss how risks affect what is important to management

☐ Speak the business language

USEFUL LINKS AND TEMPLATES

- Risk e-Views Vol 4 December 2010 – Risk Leadership: How to be Heard
  https://www.bryanwhitefield.com.au/blog/risk-e-views-vol-4-december-2010-risk-leadership-how-to-be-heard/

12. Include risk information in the company's external communication

Risk disclosure is very important. Increasingly, stakeholders are expecting companies to test and disclose the effectiveness of not only financial risk management but also other business risks, including market, operational, safety, legal etc.

When disclosing information about risks to external stakeholders, it is recommended to include at least:

- A brief statement about the company's overall commitment to risk-based planning, budgeting, project management, investment and decision-making. This information may be disclosed in the annual report and on the company's website in the section entitled "Corporate Governance".
- A more detailed statement in the annual report, including:
  - overview of the current risk-based processes,
  - the progress that has been made in integrating risks and building risk culture since last year,
  - the management structure, which contributes to the risk-based management of the company and any other significant achievements.

In the true spirit of risk management integration, it may be a good idea to spread the information about risk management throughout the annual report instead of creating a separate section titled "Risk Management". For example, risks associated with strategic objectives may be described in the Company Strategy sections, risks associated with liquidity, foreign exchange and interest rates may be described in the Financial report (most organisations already do this part), risk associated with social and environmental activities covered in the Social responsibility section etc.

The disclosure of the following information is optional: information about key risks associated with the business plan or the achievement of the strategic objectives and any information about the past incidents or losses. Keep in mind, that risk management disclosure should not include any sensitive information or trade secrets.

It is important to remember however that there may be some risks which are required to be disclosed by law.

Other external reports where risk management information may need to be disclosed:

- any fundraising activities;
- security issuer quarterly reports;
- other documents, required by stock exchanges, regulators or investors.

Finally, we would like to encourage risk managers to present at conferences and related events to talk about risk management and to raise awareness about ISO31000:2009.

USE THE CHECKLIST PROVIDED BELOW TO TURN THIS SECTION INTO ACTIONS

☐ Get involved in the preparation of external company reports. Update internal policies and procedures to take ownership over preparation of all sections related to risk management

☐ Review guidance published by central banks, stock exchanges or other legal requirements related on disclosing risk information

☐ Develop a calendar of external reports throughout the year to keep track of all obligations

☐ Present at risk management conferences and talk about risk management and raise awareness about ISO31000:2009

USEFUL VIDEOS

Alex Sidorenko from RISK-ACADEMY talks about what risk reports are useful and how to integrate risk reporting into regular management reporting
https://www.youtube.com/watch?v=AOGrobGzeaQ

I3. Include risk information into existing internal communication channels

Forget the old-fashioned risk information flows from business units to risk managers who develop risk reports and present them to executives, the audit committee or the Board. There is a better way. Based on the research and interviews we conducted, the internal risk communication should be two-way:

- Business units should be reporting on their own risks as part of normal business activities (be it weekly, monthly or quarterly performance reporting) as well as any significant decisions;
- Risk managers should be reporting on risks when there is an alternative point of view that is contradictory to business unit opinion or risk managers have additional information which should be considered when making a decision.

One thing is clear, information about risks should flow in the organisation every day and every time a decision is being made, not once a week or month when a risk assessment is done.

There are several ways to significantly improve internal risk management communication:

- Include the requirement to share / disclose risk information in policies and procedures;
- Change internal reporting templates to include risk analysis results;
- Get involved in report and document preparation to make sure risks are adequately captured;
- Create own communication channels (newsletters, intranet site, email alerts);
- Take ownership of some internal reporting on risks.

USE THE CHECKLIST PROVIDED BELOW TO TURN THIS SECTION INTO ACTIONS

- ☐ Identify existing information flows (management performance reporting, decision making / approvals, information bulletins)

- ☐ Change internal policies and procedures to require risk information to be included / disclosed

- ☐ Change existing reporting templates to include risk management information

- ☐ Provide methodologies to business units to help them accurately disclose risk information

- ☐ Review / validate results to check for quality, accuracy, consistency and completeness

14. Create simple risk escalation mechanisms

Risks rarely happen overnight. There are usually signals, warning signs. Despite their best intentions, executives and most certainly the risk manager are often detached from the operational activities. And while it should be the risk manager's goal to get involved and at least be aware of what is happening in the company, it is up to all employees to identify potential issues early and notify the risk manager.

Employees are an invaluable source of information on operational and emerging risks. Usually, junior and mid-level staff discuss emerging issues and potential threats freely long before they become public knowledge. To take advantage of this source of information, risk managers need to develop a simple and transparent mechanism for communicating and escalating risks. The company employees should be able to just make a phone call or send a confidential email or upload information to a secure intranet site to share their concern about a risk and/or any uncertainty.

It is equally important to promote these confidential channels and inform staff about their existence. Based on the interviews we have conducted, risk managers told us that while such hotlines are rarely used, their shear existence creates a trustworthy relationship between the risk manager and the business.

USE THE CHECKLIST PROVIDED BELOW TO TURN THIS SECTION INTO ACTIONS

- ☐ Build an anonymous message form on the intranet page dedicated to risk management

- ☐ If your company has a whistleblower hotline add risk management issues to the list of problems covered

- ☐ Create a dedicated email mailbox to receive information about emerging risks

- ☐ Provide training on how to use all escalation tools described above (hotline, web, email)

- ☐ Build awareness by presenting at staff meetings and developing posters to be shared around the office

USEFUL VIDEOS

Alex Sidorenko from RISK-ACADEMY talks about building trust in risk management, which is required to stay informed and up-to-date with information necessary to perform risk analysis
https://www.youtube.com/watch?v=PlRccHASvEU

OBJECTIVE 3: BECOME A TRUSTED ADVISOR

J. VALIDATE MANAGEMENT ASSUMPTIONS

Validating management assumptions is probably the single most important value a risk manager can bring to his / her company. As companies and markets are becoming more interdependent, an issue in one industry or country may have a flow on effect on the global supply chain. The business environment is becoming more volatile. Unfortunately, many companies have been slow to adjust for such volatility. We have noticed an alarming trend to match the models to the desired outcomes to keep shareholders happy and justify bonus payments. Risk management needs to be vigilant to this often unethical behaviour. These topics were very well disclosed in the Professor Patrick McNutt's book *Strategic code - patterns and prediction of behaviour.*

Management assumptions about interest rates, FX, market growth, customer behaviour and new technologies are quickly becoming outdated or overly optimistic. Risk managers play a vital role in verifying those assumptions to ensure they remain current and realistic.

Scenario analysis, stress testing and Monte-Carlo simulations help risk managers test current business plans and financial models to verify and validate assumptions made by management. Some risk managers use game theory principles and behavioural psychology to help management look at the strategic risks from different angles.

USE THE CHECKLIST PROVIDED BELOW TO TURN THIS SECTION INTO ACTIONS

☐ Perform sensitivity analysis to identify critical management assumptions made in planning, budgeting, investment analysis or project management

☐ Establish reliable external or internal sources of information to validate management assumptions

☐ Perform Monte-Carlo simulations to show how volatility affects objectives / decisions and whether management assumptions are realistic

USEFUL VIDEOS

RISK MANAGEMENT
QUICK WINS

Alex Sidorenko from RISK-ACADEMY talks about risk management quick win - testing management assumptions
https://www.youtube.com/watch?v=mGxYi6-kaoM

K. INFORM MANAGEMENT ABOUT EMERGING RISKS

Risk managers can bring a lot of value to the company by informing management about emerging risks. To do this, risk managers need to establish procedures for scanning the external and internal environment, for identifying emerging risks, recording them and informing senior management in a timely manner.

In order to identify emerging risks, risk managers need to regularly communicate with representatives from different business units. Some suggested that risk managers should establish a routine that allows them to have weekly or daily informal conversations (over coffee, group lunches, quick chats in the corridor) with the heads of different business units. One risk manager we interviewed created an informal table tennis tournament to have an opportunity to meet different business units in an informal relaxed setting every week. Another risk manager suggested joining efforts with internal auditors or internal control specialists to identify emerging risks and to provide management with an assessment of organisational readiness / resilience to meet emerging threats.

Staying connected with the global risk community is also a good way to learn about some emerging risks. Although truth be told most national risk management associations are more concerned about fashionable risks or what we may call fads. And they are often late, jumping on the bandwagon once the risk becomes imminent, not emerging.

USE THE CHECKLIST PROVIDED BELOW TO TURN THIS SECTION INTO ACTIONS

☐ Establish a routine to have regular informal conversations with business unit heads

☐ Stay up to date with latest developments in the global risk community

☐ Develop a procedure for having emerging risks discussions with management

☐ Work with internal audit to test your organisation's preparedness / readiness for emerging risks

L. PROMOTE RISK MANAGEMENT AS A SERVICE

Risk managers have a unique competency to identify and analyse risks using advanced tools like scenario analysis, sensitivity analysis, decision trees and Monte-Carlo simulations. This toolset can significantly improve business decision making. And just like any other service or tool it needs to be marketed to the rest of the organisation.

Risk management needs to be seen as an internal service offering.

Risk managers need to make management aware and to promote its quantitative risk analysis and risk modelling services to the business. Risk managers should have a clearly documented value proposition for its services, including:

- Documented methodology;
- Estimation of time and company resources;
- Expected benefits;
- Reporting templates and examples.

USE THE CHECKLIST PROVIDED BELOW TO TURN THIS SECTION INTO ACTIONS

- ☐ Develop quantitative risk analysis and modelling competencies within the risk management team

- ☐ Promote risk management competencies within the organisation using internal meeting, bulletins and corporate website

- ☐ Provide quantitative risk analysis services to different business units within the organisation

- ☐ Offer quantitative risk analysis services to key contractors, suppliers and other counterparties

USEFUL VIDEOS

RISK MANAGEMENT AS A SERVICE

Alex Sidorenko from RISK-ACADEMY talks about way how corporate risk managers can treat their work as an internal service offering.
https://www.youtube.com/watch?v=qE0NItUkIGU

M.   TAKE OWNERSHIP OVER SOME RISK ASSESSMENTS

At the risk of sounding controversial, we believe risk managers sometimes need to take responsibility for providing an independent risk analysis not based on the information provided by management. Although rare, there may be situations where management approving the project or making a decision has significant conflicts of interest or there may be suspicion of corruption.

Risk managers need to establish risk analysis methodologies that limit reliance on management information and internal data which may be tampered with. Risk analysis should be based on industry data, statistical information and external reliable providers etc.

Risk managers should also use communication channels that allow presentation of an alternative point of view to management. While the goal should be working with the business and providing the necessary support to make risk-based decisions, sometimes risk managers need to play the role of a policeman.

As a result, risk managers may be required to defend their position at the executive meetings, propose risk mitigation actions and even take responsibility for some of the risk mitigation. As someone who had to do it almost on a weekly basis, we can tell you it takes a lot of courage and bulletproof risk management methodologies. It's difficult, but it's the only way to become an equal participant in the decision making and not just an observer.

USE THE CHECKLIST PROVIDED BELOW TO TURN THIS SECTION INTO ACTIONS

- ☐ Discuss with senior management the need for an alternative / opposing point of view on certain business decisions

- ☐ Consider having veto power for risk managers on certain types of business decisions

- ☐ Develop risk analysis methodologies that do not heavily rely on management information

- ☐ Establish an independent escalation channel to raise issues if management is ignoring risks

USEFUL VIDEOS

WILL THE ROLE OF THE RISK MANAGER CHANGE?

Alex Sidorenko from RISK-ACADEMY talks about how will the role of the risk manager will change over the next few years
https://www.youtube.com/watch?v=IubYqCFiJ2c

N. BUILD YOUR OWN NETWORK OF RISK ADVISORS

We always encourage risk managers not to reinvent the wheel. Learn from others. Build connections with risk managers from similar companies. A good place to meet similar minded risk managers is the G31000 group on LinkedIn https://www.linkedin.com/groups/1834592.

Do not be afraid to share your own experiences or participate in online and face-to-face discussions or initiatives designed to promote risk management in your country. For example, help improve ISO 31000:2009 Wikipedia page or make one in your language (we have created the one in Russian language) or provide comments to your national representative in the ISO Technical Committee 262 who are currently working on updating ISO31000.

Help spread the messages in this guide by sharing it with your colleagues:

Join the RISK-ACADEMY YouTube channel to watch more videos:

https://www.youtube.com/channel/UCog9jkDZdiRps2w27MZ5Azg

O. CONTINUOUSLY IMPROVE YOUR OWN RISK MANAGEMENT SKILLS

Risk management has evolved significantly over the last 10 years and we probably haven't seen the last of the changes just yet. Norman Marks recently called for a leap change in risk management guidance. Alex Sidorenko, one of the authors of this guide, has also published a series of articles calling for a major change in risk management thinking, moving away from a stand-alone risk management process to a tool integrated into day to day decision making. Alas, it's unlikely to happen any time soon, the resistance of some old-fashioned risk managers and consultants, who have little comprehension of how risk management works in real life, is very strong, pushing back on a lot of very valid and sound ideas. And while the leap change is not likely to happen, the progress is obvious. Significant changes will come next year when the updated ISO31000 is due to be published.

Just as risk management is evolving, risk managers need to continuously build and improve their own skills as well. This means understanding the science behind how humans think in situations of uncertainty, how they behave and make decisions. Studying quantitative risk analysis tools and techniques is also becoming more and more important, given the abundance of data. And of course, understanding the company's core business, what drives its performance and applicable industry trends.

Nowadays, senior management expect risk managers to actively participate in the decision-making process, taking ownership of the risk analysis and sharing the responsibility for the decisions outcome. As a result, some risk managers need a major upgrade to their teams and their own thinking. The times of qualitative risk assessments, risk registers and heat maps are finally over.

USE THE CHECKLIST PROVIDED BELOW TO TURN THIS SECTION INTO ACTIONS

☐ Develop a skills matrix for the risk management team that should include soft skills related to ability to think independently and be stress resistant, and skills related to quantitative risk analysis, risk perception and risk psychology, core business processes and sales and marketing

☐ Consider participating in an international risk management certification programme that covers all aspects of future risk management

USEFUL VIDEOS

FOUR THINGS EVERY RISK MANAGER MUST KNOW

Alex Sidorenko from RISK-ACADEMY talks about the need to know: standards, cognitive biases, risk modelling and industry experience to be a successful risk manager.
https://www.youtube.com/watch?v=nqmnycKZwgg

HOW CAN A RISK MANAGER CONTINUE TO DEVELOP HIS SKILLS?

Alex Sidorenko from RISK-ACADEMY talks about how a modern-day risk manager can continue to grow his risk management skills
https://www.youtube.com/watch?v=X9-5rpvxtqE

WHICH RISK MANAGEMENT CERTIFICATION TO CHOOSE

Alex Sidorenko talks about 3 things to consider when choosing a risk management certification programme. He also talks about different certification options that are currently available in the market.

https://www.youtube.com/watch?v=bvV41BrqKmg

You have almost finished reading the guide and we hope you found it both enjoyable and useful. Please rate the guide and write us a short feedback

NEXT STEPS

We sincerely hope that this guide was helpful to you. Let's quickly summarise some of key points:

- Risk management is not just about tools and techniques; it is about changing the corporate culture and the mindset of management and employees. This change cannot happen overnight, risk managers need to start small by embedding elements of risk analysis into various decision making processes, expanding the scope of risk management over time.

- It is vital to break the status quo where risk management is seen as a separate and independent activity. Instead, risk managers should integrate risk management into all core business activities. This can be achieved by integrating risk analysis into decision-making processes, assisting management in evaluating projects and strategic initiatives with the use of risk analysis tools, integrating risk management into strategic planning, budgeting and performance management, incorporating responsibilities in job descriptions, providing management training and etc.

- Risk managers should strive to become advisors to senior management and the Board. Advisers that are trusted and whose recommendations are listened to. To achieve this, risk managers may need to break away from traditional models like "3 lines of defence" and instead choose to actively participate in the decision making, take ownership of some risks and provide an independent assessment of risks associated with important business decisions, maybe even veto some high-risk activities.

We have provided two indicative roadmaps that will help to prioritise the 15 points of this guide in the appendix. Risk management should divide their efforts into:

- «Here and now» – help the management to identify and manage risks that they previously neglected by integrating risk management into the most critical business processes. The good news for the risk managers (and not so good for the business): there will always be risks that are poorly managed or totally ignored by management.

- «Long-term initiatives» – developing strong risk management culture in the organisation should be the focus. Top management and employees may need time to understand positive aspects of risk management, but the results are worth it. Develop the management needed for a timely analysis of business decisions and become indispensable.

Making organisations risk aware is not quick, it's a journey. Good luck on your journey and thank you for taking the time to study this guide!

NEED MORE HELP?

RISK-ACADEMY (subsidiary of International Risk Services) provides a range of safety, risk management and environmental services globally:

https://www.risk-academy.ru/en/safety-risk-management-services/

Auditing and benchmarking

RISK-ACADEMY provides auditing and benchmarking against local legislation, ISO 45001 - Occupational Health and Safety, ISO 14000 - Environmental management, ISO 31000 - Risk management as well as other major international standards and guidelines. Independent gap analysis against legislative and standardization requirements.

Design and implementation

ISO 45001, ISO 14000, ISO 31000 system development and implementation. Integrated risk, safety and environmental management is a positive signal to stakeholders and investors. Direct saving from risk management far outweigh the cost of implementation.

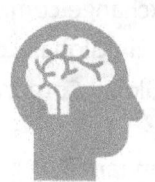

Risk assessments

RISK-ACADEMY provides numerous strategic, investment, plant, manual handling and working at heights risk assessments for large, medium and small sized companies. Our team is able to perform risk management modelling on individual projects or the portfolio of projects. We use latest Palisade Decision Tools software for Monte Carlo simulations.

Outsourced risk management

RISK-ACADEMY provide ongoing risk management and safety support to organizations who don't want to keep a fulltime staff dedicated to risk management. We offer clients annual packages to provide experienced risk management professionals to be available on call.

BIBLIOGRAPHY

- AM Best and Towers Perrin (2008). AM Best ERM criteria. www.towersperrin.com
- Australian Securities Exchange, 2007. Principles of Corporate Governance and Best Practice Recommendations. www.asx.com.au
- Buchanan, D.A. and Huczynski, A. (2010), Organisational Behaviour, 7th ed., Pearson Education Ltd.
- Carey, A. (2004), Corporate Governance. A Practical Guide. [online].London Stock Exchange plc & RSM Robson Rhodes LLP., London. http://www.londonstockexchange.com.
- Chryssides, G. and Kaler, J. (1996), Essentials of Business Ethics, McGraw-Hill International (UK) Limited, England.
- Davies, H. and Lam, P.L. (2001) Managerial economics. 3rd ed., Bell & Bain Ltd., Glasgow.
- Deloitte. (2006). Risk Intelligence in the Age of Global Uncertainty. Prudent Preparedness for Myriad Threats.
- Demidenko, E. and McNutt, P. (2010), "The ethics of enterprise risk management as a key component of corporate governance" International Journal of SocialEconomics, Vol. 37 No. 10, pp. 802-815. http:// www.emeraldinsight.com/0306-8293.htm
- Economist Intelligence Unit. (2009), Managing risk in Managing risk in perilous times. Practical steps to accelerate recovery. http://www.eiu.com
- European Corporate Governance Institute (n.d.), Codes of Corporate Governance in different countries. http://www.ecgi.org/codes/all_codes.php.
- European Union (2006), "Article 41. Audit Committee", 8th Company Law Directive 2006/43/EC (2006). http://www.8th-company-law- directive.com/Article41.htm.
- Expert RA (2010), Risk Management System Quality Rating, www.raexpert.ru/ratings/risk/scale/
- Hampel Committee on Corporate Governance (2003), The Combined Code on Corporate Governance. London Stock Exchange, London. http://www.londonstockexchange.com.
- Hickson, D.J. and Pugh, D. (2003), Management Worldwide. 2nd ed., Penguin Global, London.
- International corporate governance network (2005), ICGN Statement on Global Corporate Governance Principles. http://www.icgn.org.
- ISO (2009). Risk management - principles and guidelines. International Standard 31000. First edition 2009-11-15, ISO, Switzerland
- IFRS (2010). IFRS 4 Phase II, Exposure Draft Insurance Contracts. www. ifrs.org
- KPMG (2009). Never again? Risk management in banking beyond the credit crisis. http://www.kpmg.com
- KPMG. (2011). Risk Management. A Driver of Enterprise Value in the Emerging Environment. http://www.kpmg.com
- Lam, J. (2003) Enterprise Risk Management: from incentives to controls, John Wiley & Sons, Inc., New Jersey.
- Marks, N. (2015) World-Class Risk Management, CreateSpace Independent Publishing
- McNutt, P. (2005), Law, Economics and Antitrust, Edward Elgar Publications, Cheltenham, UK.
- McNutt, P (2013) "Decoding strategy - Pattern and predictions", McGraw-Hill Education (Asia); 2 edition
- McNutt, P. and Batho, C. (2005), "Code of Ethics and Employee Governance", International Journal of Social Economics, VOL.32 No.8, pp656-666.

- McKinsey&Company. (2011) Governance since the economic crisis. Global survey results. http://www.mckinsey.com
- Monks, R. and Minow, N. (2003), Corporate Governance. 3rd ed., Blackwell Publishing, Oxford.
- New York Stock Exchange (2003) Standards for Corporate Governance 303A.09 http://www.nyse.com/Frameset.html; http://www.nyse.com/about/listed/1101074746736.html; http://www.nyse.com/pdfs/section303A_final_rules.pdf
- PriceWaterhouseCoopers and Centre for Study of Financial Innovation. (2010). Banking Banana Skins 2010. Russia. http://www.pwc.ru
- RBCC (2006), Capital Markets: The next move for Russian business Bulletin, Issue. 3, February, pp. 24-25.
- Ricketts, M. (2002), The Economics of Business Enterprise An Introduction to Economic Organisation and the Theory of the Firm, 3rd ed., Elgar Publishing.
- Risk e-Views Vol 4, December 2010, Risk Leadership: How to be Heard, Bryan Whitefield, Director, Risk Management Partners
- Standard and Poor's. (2010) Approach To Assessing Insurers' Enterprise Risk Management Refined In Line With Industry Improvements, RatingsDirect on the Global Credit Portal, www.standardandpoors.com/ratingsdirect
- Standard and Poor's. (2010) Expanded Definition Of Adequate Classification In Enterprise Risk Management Scores, RatingsDirect on the Global Credit Portal, www.standardandpoors.com/ratingsdirect
- Standard and Poor's. (2010) Insurers In EMEA See The Value Of Enterprise Risk Management. RatingsDirect on the Global Credit Portal, www.standardandpoors.com/ratingsdirec
- The Banking Committee on Banking Supervision, (2010), Basel III and Financial Stability. http://www.bis.org
- The Committee of European Insurance and Occupational Pensions Supervisors (CEIOPS), (2009). Solvency II Directive. http://ec.europa.eu/internal_market/insurance/solvency
- The Russian Federal Commission for Stock Markets (2003), The FCSM Code for Corporate Governance [online]. www.fcsm.ru; www.copr-gov.ru.
- The Institute of Internal Auditors. 2004. The Role of Internal Auditing in Enterprise- wide Risk Management. [online], FL USA., September: www.theiia.org
- Towers Perrin (2008). Highlights and Implications of A.M. Best's New ERM Methodology.
- Vedomosti (2005), "Russia: Going Global", Forum, The Wall Street Journal & Financial Times Magazine, November.
- Vysotskaya, O. and Demidenko, E. (2005), "The Audit Committees in the 21st century". The Russian Economy. 21st century. No. 20. http://www.ruseconomy.ru/index20.html.
- World Economic Forum (2011). Global risks 2011, Sixth Edition. www.weforum.org

ABOUT THE AUTHORS

ALEX SIDORENKO, CT31000, CRMP.RR

Alex Sidorenko is an expert with over 13 years of strategic, innovation, risk and performance management experience across Australia, Russia, Poland and Kazakhstan. **In 2014 Alex was named the Risk Manager of the Year by the Russian Risk Management Association.**

As a Board member of the Institute for Strategic Risk Analysis in Decision Making (ISAR) Alex is responsible for risk management training and certification across Russia and CIS, running numerous risk management classroom and e-learning training programmes. Alex represents the Russian risk management community at the ISO Technical Committee 262 which has been responsible for the update of ISO31000:20XX and Guide 73 since 2015.

Alex is the co-author of the global PwC risk management methodology, the author of the risk management guidelines for SME (Russian standardisation organisation), risk management textbook (Russian Ministry of Finance), risk management guide (Australian Stock Exchange) and the award-winning training course on risk management (best risk education programme 2013, 2014 and 2015).

Alex worked as a Head of Risk Management at RUSNANO, one of the largest private equity funds in Russia, specialising in technology investment. Alex won an award for best ERM implementation at RUSNANO in 2014. Prior to that Alex worked in senior risk roles at Skolkovo Foundation, Strategy Partners, PwC and Deloitte.

In 2012 Alex created Risk-academy www.risk-academy.ru a web portal dedicated to free risk management training for SME across Russia and CIS.

Alex recently published his second risk management book called ***Effective Risk Management 2.0***. Alex also regularly presents at risk management conferences in Russia and Europe. In November 2012 Alex shot a series of TV programmes dedicated to risk management in start-ups. Alex teaches risk management at major Russian business schools including OpUS, Technopark Skolkovo, MIRBIS, MFUA, SKOLKOVO and USIB as well as corporate universities, like Gazprom.

He has successfully completed his double Bachelor degree in Risk Management and Econometrics at Monash University, Australia, achieving the top risk management and statistics student award two years in a row.

More information can be found here:

- http://ru.linkedin.com/in/alexsidorenko
- www.slideshare.net/AlexSidorenko/
- https://www.youtube.com/user/alexausrisk/videos

ELENA DEMIDENKO, ACCA, MBA, CT31000

Elena is a business advisor on risk management, lean management and performance management. She is a director with 10 years of experience in consulting and 18 years of combined experience in Singapore, Australia, Russia and Europe. Elena pioneered the development of risk management in Russia in 2005, and is a member of the official translation of COSO ERM into the Russian language. Elena has successful experience in managing large-scale projects on risk management development and implementation, business transformations, including change management, profitability increase and she has worked with large financial institutions, and non-financial companies and government departments. Elena has conducted risk management projects from outside and within companies. During these projects Elena has successfully conducted training for senior management as well as effectively facilitated "kaizen sessions" working groups and strategic risk assessment seminars.

Elena is also a member of the teaching staff at Manchester Business School, UK. She is the co-author and professor of the course, which includes the questions of ethics and responsibility in business, risk management and corporate governance, competition policy and antitrust laws and the theory of games.

Elena is the author of several publications on corporate governance and risk management, including the publication of her book on risk management ***Becoming a valuable risk manager - risk management guide*** in November 2012. She published the article "*The ethics of enterprise risk management as a key component of corporate governance*" for the International Journal of SocialEconomics, Vol. 37 No. 10 in October 2010 and the article "*Audit Committees in the 21st century*" in 2005.

www.ingramcontent.com/pod-product-compliance
Lightning Source LLC
Chambersburg PA
CBHW081729170526
45167CB00009B/3761